Sewing *the* New Classics

Sewing *the* New Classics

~ Clothes *with* Easy Style

Carol Parks

Sterling Publishing Co., Inc. **New York**
A Sterling/Lark Book

Art Direction: **Chris Bryant**

Illustrations: **Kay Holmes Stafford, Chris Bryant**

Production: **Chris Bryant**

Editorial Assistance: **Susan Kieffer, Marjolyn Nordhorn**

Production Assistance: **Neil Thomas, Resource Data**

Library of Congress Cataloging-in-Publication Data

Parks, Carol.
    Sewing the new classics : clothes with easy style / by Carol Parks.
      p. cm.
    "A Sterling/Lark Book."
    Includes index.
    ISBN 0–8069–3193–0
    1. Tailoring (Women's) 2. Machine sewing. I. Title.
TT519.5.P37 1995
646.4'04 — dc20   95-20037
                                  CIP

10 9 8 7 6 5 4 3 2 1

A Sterling/Lark Book

Published in 1995 by Sterling Publishing Co., Inc.
387 Park Avenue South, New York, NY 10016

Produced by Altamont Press, Inc.
50 College Street, Asheville, NC 28801

Text and photos credited on page 142 © 1995 by Altamont Press

Patterns © Knipmode/Uitgeverij Spaarnestad BV, Haarlem, Holland.

Photos not credited on page 142 © Knipmode, Libelle, Margriet/Uitgeverij Spaarnestad, Haarlem, Holland.

Distributed in Canada by Sterling Publishing,
c/o Canadian Manda Group, One Atlantic Ave., Suite 105, Toronto, Ontario M6K 3E7

Distributed in Great Britain and Europe by Cassell PLC
Wellington House, 125 Strand, London WC2R 0BB, England

Distributed in Australia by Capricorn Link (Australia) Pty Ltd.
P.O. Box 6651, Baulkham Hills Business Centre, NSW 2153, Australia

Printed in Hong Kong.

ISBN 0-8069-3193-0

Contents

INTRODUCTION

A GOOD BASIC GARMENT PATTERN

should be taken with a grain of salt. It should serve just as a starting point for the sewer's own original creation. It should have simple lines to allow for easy fitting and to accommodate the sewer's design changes.

The patterns presented here were chosen for their clean lines and timeless styling. They are clothes meant to be worn with pleasure for several years, not discarded after a single season. And they can be combined in endless ways to make up a good-looking and dependable wardrobe.

The photos suggest all kinds of variations, but they are only a sampling

of those you'll invent on your own once you begin to think of the pattern as only a beginning. We encourage you to take liberties with the patterns and adapt them in any way that pleases you. Add new seamlines. Add pleats or tabs. Experiment with your own pocket design or an unusual belt. Try embroidery or fabric painting. Piece or pleat the fabric before you cut.

A good pattern begins with a good fit. Once any necessary alterations are made, it can be used over and over again and never produce exactly the same results. Changes in fabric colors and textures, slight alteration of a seamline here and there, addition

of a design detail, a little embellishment, and the one pattern can provide dozens of very different garments.

Most of us sooner or later develop our own sense of style, a combination of what suits our day-to-day lives, the colors that flatter and please us, fabrics we find comfortable, and designs that suit our personalities.

As sewers, we can have it all. We are not restricted to this year's unmanageable hem length or peculiar color offerings. We don't have to settle for poor fabric quality or inferior workmanship. We can place the pockets where we like them, have a zipper

ABCDEFGHIJ

instead of buttons, or add a lining for wearing comfort.

This approach to sewing is somewhat different than the buy-a-pattern, sew-it-up, hope-it-looks-like-the-picture method many of us have always employed. Please take time to read the section on working with the patterns, and take a little more time to stitch up and fit a test garment for your pattern. Then use the photos for ideas, and create a beautiful wardrobe that's uniquely yours.

A NOTE ABOUT MEASUREMENTS

MEASUREMENTS THROUGHOUT THE BOOK ARE GIVEN BOTH IN INCHES AND CENTIMETERS. EXACT CONVERSION FROM ONE SYSTEM TO THE OTHER OFTEN RESULTS IN FRACTIONS THAT ARE IMPOSSIBLE TO MEASURE; THEREFORE, ADJUSTMENTS HAVE BEEN MADE IN ORDER TO PRESENT THE MEASUREMENTS IN A WORKABLE FORM. FOR THIS REASON IT IS VERY IMPORTANT TO CHOOSE ONE SYSTEM OF MEASUREMENT OR THE OTHER, THEN TO STAY WITH IT THROUGHOUT A PROJECT.

Tools and Equipment

Sewing Area

An organized, well-equipped, and comfortable work area allows you to concentrate on the creative aspects of sewing. Even if it's just a small corner, or a room that doubles as a guest room or study, a sewing space that is set up efficiently will make your project more enjoyable.

Good lighting is essential, not just at the machine, but over the ironing board too. Clamp-on lights with flexible arms are very inexpensive and many can accommodate a 100-watt bulb.

Lack of an adequate place to cut out is a common sewing room complaint. Discount office supply stores sell long folding tables that allow you to lay out an entire garment at one time. Bricks or blocks under the legs elevate the table to a comfortable height for back-ache-free cutting.

Sewing Machine

It need not be a state-of-the-art model, but it must produce a good stitch and be able to handle a variety of fabrics with aplomb. Most machines—given regular care—will do this. Even the most expensive, sophisticated model will not perform well without regular cleaning and oiling and periodic adjustment of its mechanical parts.

A good rule of thumb is to clean lint from the machine, oil it according to the manual instructions, and change the needle at the start of each project. If you sew almost daily (lucky you!), then brush out the lint and check oil needs at the end of each day's sewing.

NEEDLES

The most important part of a sewing machine is the needle. It is also the least expensive part, and the easiest part to replace. Yet more sewing machine problems can be traced to a faulty needle that to any other single cause! It is essential to replace the needle regularly, and to use the correct type.

Machine needles are categorized in three different ways: the type, the size, and the point style.

The needle *type* your machine uses depends upon the brand and vintage of the machine. It will be specified in the owner's manual and often imprinted on the machine itself. Using the wrong needle type will result in terrible stitch quality and can actually damage the machine.

The needle *size* is determined by the fabric you will be sewing—smaller needles for lightweight fabrics and larger ones for heavy or dense material. Sizes are designated numerically, lower numbers for smaller, finer needles, and higher numbers for larger needles. European-made needles range from 60 to 120 and American needles from about 10 to 20. Most packages will be marked both ways, i.e. 80/12 for a medium-size needle.

The needle's *point style* also should suit the fabric being sewn. Unless the package indicates otherwise, the needles have a very slightly rounded or "universal" point, and are suitable for a variety of sewing jobs. Ballpoint needles are necessary for sewing knits and elastic; a sharper point can puncture threads of the fabric and create a hole or run. Sharp needles, sometimes packaged as "jeans" needles, are the best choice for very tightly woven fabrics like sandwashed silk, microfibers, cotton poplin and broadcloth, and of course heavy denim. They are available in a range of sizes. If a universal needle performs like a dull needle—causing a popping sound as it pulls out of the fabric or pulling threads along the stitching line—then a sharp needle might be needed.

In addition to the basic point styles and sizes above, there are all sorts of needles designed for specialized tasks and materials. The topstitching needle has a larger eye and larger thread groove to accommodate thicker topstitching thread, making it unnecessary to change to a larger needle size that might be unsuitable for a finer fabric. The leather needle has a chisel-like point which leaves a slit rather than a visible hole where it pierces the material. It is not meant for synthetic suede and leather fabrics. As new fabrics and fabric finishes are developed, new sewing machine needles come along to sew them efficiently.

Many needles are designed just for decorative sewing. With double and triple needles, some very unusual effects can result from simple straight stitching. The wing needle simulates hand hemstitching. And there are specialized needles for machine quilting, embroidery, and for use with metallic threads.

It's a good idea to keep an assortment of needles on hand. It's easy, then, to use the one best suited for your project. And it will prevent you from becoming a needle miser.

PRESSER FEET

As with needles, the use of presser feet tailored to certain tasks can eliminate much sewing difficulty and produce better results. If you tend to keep the all-purpose presser foot in place except when installing a zipper, take out your machine manual, review the functions of the feet that came with your machine, and stitch a practice swatch with each one. Then visit the dealer to see what's new. Most machine manufacturers have introduced a variety of special-purpose presser feet in the past few years to keep pace with innovations in materials and techniques. If you are having difficulty with a particular fabric or technique, the dealer may be able to solve your problem with a new presser foot.

For garment making, there are several presser feet that are especially useful. The *multi-motion* foot is designed for use with stitches created by a side-to-side needle movement combined with alternating forward/reverse fabric feed. The specialized foot prevents the needle thread catching on the front of the foot, and allows the foot to slip easily over previous stitching during the reverse feed phase of the stitch formation.

A *straight stitch foot* makes for neater topstitching, and works well for seams in light fabrics that have a tendency to disappear into the needle hole of the stitch plate. For real problem situations, a straight stitch throat plate provides even better control of such fabrics.

The *blind hemmer* is an accessory ignored by many sewers. Mastering it does take some practice, but it then becomes indispensable. The most common complaint—an indentation on the right side of the fabric along the stitching line—is often cured by adjusting upper thread tension.

The *edge stitch foot* keeps topstitching parallel with the fabric edge. With an overcast foot, seam allowances of even lightweight fabric can be overcast without a ridge forming along the edge.

The *roller foot* and *walking foot* are helpful in situations where fabric layers tend to feed unevenly, such as corduroy, velvet, knits, and fabrics layered for quilting. The walking foot is better for severe cases, and when an exact match at seamlines is essential, as with plaids. It is also more expensive, and a rewarding investment.

A *Teflon-coated foot* slides easily over "sticky" fabrics like synthetic suede and heavily finished decorating cottons. For many machines, both the basic foot and zipper foot are available with Teflon coating.

There are many other special-purpose presser feet that perform well at certain tasks. The *piping foot* for stitching and applying corded piping, *cording foot*, and *gathering feet* all are time-savers. Dozens of other feet, each used for a specific decorative sewing technique, are very helpful when your project involves that technique.

Serger

The serger, or overlock machine, was originally developed for industrial use. Its adoption by home sewers is fairly recent—and very enthusiastic. A serger can sew a seam, trim it, and overcast the edges in a single pass through the machine. And it sews about 20 percent faster than a good sewing machine.

A serger can cut in half the time spent on tedious sewing tasks such as trimming seams, overcasting edges, hemming facings, and so forth. It does a great job with knit fabrics, which tend to ripple less when serger-sewn.

The same care should be given a serger as a sewing machine. Needles should be changed regularly and it must be oiled from time to time. A serger produces a great deal of lint, so should be cleaned frequently. The lower knife blade needs to be replaced from time to time, or immediately if it's nicked from sewing over a pin.

Sewing Equipment and Tools

A favorite sewing book published nearly 40 years ago lists 31 items under this same heading as essential for a well-equipped sewing room. In the latest catalog from a mail-order notions supplier are more than 120 *pages* of findings and gadgets and supplies intended to speed up or simplify the sewing process, or contribute in some way toward production of a top-quality garment.

No two sewers on earth would come up with the same list of "essential" sewing aids. These are our favorites, some of which are essential only some of the time.

CUTTING AND LAYOUT EQUIPMENT

DRESSMAKER'S SHEARS

Use them only for fabric, never for paper. Have them sharpened occasionally; synthetic fabrics also will dull the blades.

TRIMMING SCISSORS

Look for short, thick, pointed blades which allow good control when cutting through multiple layers.

PINKING SHEARS

Still the best bet for a clean finish on seam allowances where an overcast stitch would be too bulky. They should not be used to cut out the garment.

ROTARY CUTTING SYSTEM: CUTTING WHEEL, GRIDDED MAT, SEE-THROUGH RULER

If you haven't yet used these tools, you have a treat in store! Weights, instead of pins, keep the pattern and fabric in place, so there is no distortion of the pieces, and no time wasted pinning and unpinning. For this reason it's a great system for accurate cutting of slippery fabrics – linings and lightweight silks – that often have wavy edges when cut with shears. Used with a ruler, the cutter does a quick, accurate job with straight pieces such as waistbands, facings, etc. The cutter can be purchased with an attached guide that allows for adding seam allowance as fabric is cut.

CARDBOARD CUTTING MAT

One that folds for storage, printed with a 1" grid, is also handy for laying out pattern pieces to figure yardage requirements, and for straightening the grain of fabric pieces.

MEASURING TOOLS

TAPE MEASURE

The spring-return style, accurately marked, is best. Many are 1/2" to 5/8" wide and can also be used along a pattern edge to add seam allowance.

CARPENTER'S SQUARE OR L-SQUARE

Use for measuring and marking perpendicular lines.

FLEXIBLE RULER

Available from drafting and art supply stores. Bend it to the desired shape, then draw along the edge.

DRESSMAKER'S CURVE OR FRENCH CURVE

It is a ruler with varying degrees of curve, useful for creating smooth curved lines when altering patterns.

SEAM/HEM GAUGE

Make sure it has a sliding marker.

EXPANDING METAL SEWING GAUGE.

It divides a line into equal segments to quickly mark buttonholes and pleats, for example.

PINS AND NEEDLES

PINS

Best are long, sharp "silk" pins with glass heads that are visible among fabric folds and won't melt when touched with a hot iron.

PINCUSHION

The magnetic kind will catch pins tossed in its general direction. Keep it away from computerized machine disks and cartridges.

HAND SEWING NEEDLES

Keep a variety, and discard the dull ones periodically.

PRESSING EQUIPMENT

STEAM IRON

A reliable one that doesn't drip is as important to sewing success as the sewing machine itself.

IRONING BOARD

For sewing, a cotton cover is better than the slippery scorch-resistant variety, as the garment will stay in place as you press.

SLEEVE BOARD

Resembling a miniature ironing board, it is handy for pressing any small area or detail.

PRESSING CLOTH

Helpful when ironing delicate fabrics and for fusing interfacings.

PRESSING HAM

A firmly stuffed form for pressing curved seams and darts.

POINT PRESSER/POUNDING BLOCK

This unusually shaped wooden tool aids in pressing hard-to-reach seams and corners, and is useful for pressing seams open without leaving an imprint on the garment's right side.

EXCELLENT GADGETS

SEAM RIPPER, OR UN-SEWING TOOL

Also used for cutting buttonholes. Replace it when it becomes dull.

TUBE TURNERS

Best is the kind that consists of a sturdy brass tube with a spiral-tipped wire to pull fabric through it; it is available in several diameters.

LOOP TURNER

It has a latchet hook at one end and is effective with very narrow fabric tubes such as those made for loop buttonholes.

POINT TURNER

It is an inexpensive plastic gadget that is better for the job than scissors points, and much safer.

POCKET TEMPLATE

It makes perfectly even corners in a choice of shapes. A clip holds fabric in place while you press.

PAPER TAPE, OR SURGICAL TAPE

Originally made for medical use and quickly adopted by sewers. Because it doesn't melt or crumple when touched with a warm iron, it is the best for altering and repairing patterns. It is easy to remove from fabric, and it doesn't leave a residue.

MARKING TOOLS

There is an incredible array of products designed to mark fabrics or keep them in place, with new ones on the market hourly. Any liquid, or any colored or sticky substance, should be tested first on every piece of fabric with which it is used. Manufacturers test their products, but there is no way to determine a product's reaction to all possible combinations of fabric, dye, and surface finishing agents. It is wise to test the substance on your fabric, then iron, and even wash, the sample.

That way you can avoid unpleasant surprises.

CHALK WHEELS

Use to mark very fine lines that will rub off easily. They are available in several colors; some can be refilled.

FELT TIP FABRIC MARKING PENS

Marks usually will rub away with a wet fingertip or cloth. Marks should be removed before laundering the article with chlorine bleach, which can set them permanently. Marks may be difficult to remove from fabrics of certain colors; always test.

TRACING WHEEL AND DRESSMAKER'S CARBON

Use it on the fabric's wrong side. A double tracing wheel can mark the pattern seamline and cutting line simultaneously.

STICKY SUBSTANCES

LIQUID FRAY RETARDANT

Rescues corners clipped too enthusiastically, and preserves edges of fabrics that fray. It can stiffen the fabric slightly.

GLUE STICK, FABRIC GLUE, BASTING LIQUID, AND BASTING ADHESIVE SHEETS

All are designed to eliminate the tedium of basting. All are helpful in certain situations.

About Fabrics

The success of a garment depends as much on a smart choice of fabric as upon careful fitting and sewing. The fabric must be compatible with the design and function of the proposed garment. Sturdy denim, for example, is too stiff and sporty a fabric for a blouse with full sleeves and a gathered yoke. Cotton lawn or silk crepe would be beautiful for this blouse, but wouldn't do for a pair of jeans.

The fabric's care requirements should be considered too. For a special outfit that might be worn twice a year during the holidays, a fussy dry-clean-only fabric isn't a problem, but for a white summer shirt that goes with absolutely everything you own it's nice to use a fabric that can withstand frequent laundering and occasional bleaching, and that requires minimal ironing. Don't create a monster that will cost you more in maintenance time than you want to give it.

Try to visualize your chosen fabric as a finished piece of clothing. Hold it in front of you and look in a mirror. Handle it to see whether it feels like something you would want to wear. Best of all, take along your most outspoken friend when you shop for fabric.

Every piece of fabric has a personality of its own. Each has a unique "hand", or feel. Each drapes in a particular way, responds differently to shaping, and has a different degree of crispness or softness. Every fabric has certain care requirements. And each will wear differently with regard to comfort and appearance.

When you buy a fabric you haven't sewn before, experiment with it a little before you start work on a garment. Decide which pressing technique works best, try different interfacings to find the best combination, and test different stitches and different length and width settings. Get to know the fabric before cutting out the garment.

The following section describes some of the most often-used garment fabrics. A little fabric savvy will help you make the best choice for the design you plan and can reward you with an attractive and comfortable garment.

A FABRIC is classified by three different means: the manner in which it is constructed, the weave or surface patterning, and the fiber from which it is made. Generally speaking, fabrics are either knitted or woven.

Knitted fabrics—jersey, handmade sweater woolens, polyester double knits, whatever—are all constructed in essentially the same way, by a series of interlocking loops. Single knits resemble the fabric of hand knitted sweaters, with the face of the fabric different in appearance from the reverse side. These fabrics often tend to curl toward the right side—an attractive feature at the neckline of a sweater, perhaps, but aggravating to cut and sew. Double knits are the same on both sides. They are more stable than comparable single knit fabrics and are easier to work with.

Knit fabrics can be made of many different fibers and may be finished in a number of different ways. Because of

FABRICS VS. FIBERS

their construction, knits require some special preparation and sewing techniques. These are described on pages 37 and 38.

Woven fabrics are often identified by their weave structure and/or surface texture, such as satin, velvet, crepe, or gabardine. Gabardine, for example, can be made of any number of different fibers, such as rayon, cotton, polyester, wool, or silk. "Gabardine" refers only to the fabric's characteristic twill weave, not to the fiber from which the fabric is made. "Velvet" describes just the appearance of the fabric, not the fiber from which it is made.

From the sewer's viewpoint, the fiber content of a fabric is its most important feature. That is what determines how to deal with the fabric during construction, how to press it, how it will perform as the garment you plan

for it, and the kind of care the finished garment will require. Fibers are the raw materials from which fabrics are made.

Fabric fibers are either natural or man-made, depending upon their origin. Natural fibers come from plants or animals—cotton, wool, silk, linen, and ramie. Man-made or synthetic fibers, such as polyester, nylon, and acrylic, are made from chemical compounds. Rayon is somewhat of a hybrid. It is a man-made fiber that comes from cellulose, a natural material. A "blend" can be any combination of fibers making up a fabric, but most often refers to the combination of a natural fiber with a synthetic.

Understanding the characteristics of different fibers and fabrics will improve your sewing skills. Any sewing project will go more smoothly if you work with the natural characteristics of your fabric rather than trying to counteract them.

The Natural Fibers

Fabrics made from natural fibers have aesthetic qualities which cannot be duplicated synthetically. Natural fibers "breathe" better than synthetics, making them cooler to wear in warm weather, warmer in cold weather. For a sewer, natural fiber fabrics are usually easier to work with than synthetics. Most are obedient and more responsive to pressing and shaping.

Virtually all natural fiber fabrics are washable, even wool and most silks—and nearly all of them will shrink in the process. These fabrics must be preshrunk if they are to be used for garments that will be washed. Washing also will remove surface finishes, leaving some fabrics completely changed in texture and appearance. The results aren't always predictable. Smoothly finished wools and heavy silks are usually best dry cleaned for this reason.

Ready-to-wear garments made of natural fibers are often labeled "Dry clean only" even though the fabric

itself is perfectly washable, because the fabric has not been preshrunk before manufacturing. In addition, interfacing or lining can shrink at a different rate than the outer fabric, resulting in rippled collars, front bands, or cuffs.

COTTON

The most versatile of all fibers, cotton produces fabrics of every conceivable weave and finish, in every texture and weight, and in every price range. Cotton fabrics are easy to sew and press, and adapt to almost any sewing technique.

Cotton often is blended with other fibers, such as polyester, to reduce wrinkling, but the blends lack the responsive qualities of pure cotton fabrics.

All cottons are washable. Most will shrink to a greater or lesser degree, so they should always be washed before use. Some cottons, especially low-priced varieties and those intended for use in home decorating, are treated with finishing agents, such as starch, to give them smoothness and stability, or render them soil or stain resistant. Washing removes the finish and leaves the fabric softer, less smooth, and with less body.

Cottons, as a group, have no special sewing and care requirements. Very tightly woven cotton, such as poplin, and very dense and tough cotton like denim, may require a sharp machine needle rather than a universal point. The size should be chosen according to the thickness of the fabric. Bright and dark-colored cotton fabrics will better retain their colors if washed in cool water and pressed on the wrong side.

Cotton Fabrics

Batiste and *lawn* are very lightweight, even-weave cottons. They are beautiful in their own right, and make exceptionally good support fabrics when used as underlining.

Flannel, or *flannelette*, is a lightweight fabric with a pronounced nap on one side. It tends to shrink considerably, so should be machine washed and dried at least once before cutting. Cotton flannel can be used as an underlining for added body or warmth.

Fox Fibre™ is a relatively new type of cotton that is not dyed but is actually grown in colors that deepen with repeated washing. Its shades range from beige to reddish-brown.

Indian cotton is a broad term that refers to lightweight fabrics made from short staple cotton fibers. They are cool and comfortable in hot weather, and are quite inexpensive. They are usually heavily finished, and will become softer and less stable when washed. Pre-shrinking is essential.

Muslin is a very versatile, very inexpensive, and highly underrated fabric, nicely suited to dyeing, fabric manipulation, and all sorts of embellishment. It develops an interesting texture when washed and machine dried. And it is available in almost any fabric store.

Organdy is a sheer, firm cotton with built-in crispness that makes it an excellent interfacing when support is needed, such as in shirt collars and under buttonholes.

Pima is the Cadillac of cottons. It has a silky hand and almost whistles when stroked. It is made from a variety of the cotton plant which produces long fibers, and which is more expensive to produce. Pima cotton fabrics tend to be crisper and more stable than fabrics from short-staple cottons. They wrinkle less, and they shrink less.

Polished cotton is a plain weave cotton, such as broadcloth, that has been chemically finished to give it sheen and crispness. The finish will not withstand laundering, but may last through several dry cleanings. Chintz is a polished cotton, usually printed with a floral pattern.

Sateen has a sheen similar to that of polished cotton, but in sateen it is due to the satin weave of the fabric, not to finishing agents, therefore will retain its appearance through washing.

Velvet, or *velveteen* made of cotton is widely available, although it also is made of rayon, silk, and wool. Cotton velvets do not have the draping qualities of rayon and silk, but are easier to sew, less expensive, and in some cases are washable.

LINEN

The fiber comes from the flax plant, and produces an extremely strong and durable fabric. Because of the complicated manufacturing process it is often fairly expensive. It is a very comfortable summer fabric because it breathes well and dries quickly.

Linen ages gracefully; the more it is used and laundered, the softer and more lustrous it becomes. White or natural colored linens can withstand washing in hot water with bleach, but dyed linens should be treated more gently to keep their colors from fading.

Linen *will* wrinkle—it's that quality which separates the real thing from the imitations. Linen that is washed wrinkles in a different way from linen that is dry cleaned. Washing leaves linen softer and somewhat rumply. New, and dry cleaned, linen fabric will crease instead. Wrinkles and all, linen has a distinctive and handsome appearance synthetic fibers can't duplicate.

Linen is available in many textures and weights. Some linen fabrics are very light and smooth, like handkerchief linen, while others are dense and sturdy enough to use for upholstery. Heavier linens often have slubs and a much rougher texture, the characteristic "linen weave" we associate with the fabric.

Linen is a *fiber*, however, not a weave. Fabrics labelled as "linen weave" or "linen look" invariably are *not* linen, but often blends of rayon and polyester. Beyond appearance, from a distance at least, the two fabrics have nothing in common. There is no such thing as "synthetic linen".

Linen should be prewashed, at least once, if it is to become a washable garment. It is a good idea to machine dry the fabric to preshrink it, then line dry the finished garment. Many sewers have linen fabric dry cleaned before making a garment which will be dry cleaned.

Linens are wonderful to sew. The heavy, tough fabrics may require a sharp "jeans" needle, number 90/14 or even 100/16. Care should be taken when sewing across thick seams. With dark-colored fabrics, press on the wrong side or use a pressing cloth to prevent shiny spots. Very lightweight handkerchief linen is easier to control if it is given a light coating of spray starch before sewing. Press with a cooler iron, then, to avoid scorching.

RAMIE

Ramie—no relation to rayon—also is a plant fiber. It produces a fabric similar to linen but somewhat coarser, not quite as durable, and less costly. It can be treated in the same way as linen or cotton, and usually is blended with one or the other in fabrics.

SILK

Silk fibers produce fabrics unsurpassed for elegance and luxurious appearance. Many silk fabrics have an inherent stiffness which allows them to drape and fold in a distinctive way, many are very soft and light, and others are rough-textured and heavy. Silk is comfortable to wear; the lightweight varieties feel delicious next to the skin.

Silk doesn't have good fabric "memory". It may stretch, but not return to its original shape. A shaped silk garment, such as a jacket, is best underlined with very light fusible interfacing like tricot or weft insertion, or with a rayon cool-fuse variety.

Lighter weight silks, such as crepe, charmeuse, and noil, wash beautifully, and become softer with time. They *will* shrink, so the fabric must be preshrunk to make a washable garment. Silk doesn't hold dye well. Dark or bright colors may fade or run when washed. These should be dry cleaned to keep the colors intact, or if washed, washed alone. Heavy silks also should be dry cleaned to retain their finish.

Silk should be washed with a gentle soap, not detergent. Best is a livestock shampoo, available at farm supply stores and from quilting and yarn suppliers. Regular shampoo, without conditioner or the like, also is good.

Lightweight silks, crepe and charmeuse for example, should be sewn with a fine universal-point needle – a brand new one in perfect condition. Since the slightest nick in the needle point can pull a thread in the fabric, it's a good idea to change to a new needle before doing the final topstitching or making the buttonholes on a delicate garment.

Suit-weight silks like matka and tussah may require a medium-sized sharp needle. These fabrics are very strong!

Sandwashed silks present some challenges for the sewer. They appear delicate but in fact are quite tough. A universal point needle often will pull threads in the same way a dull needle will do. If this happens, use a sharp needle, often packaged as "jeans" needles, in size 70/10 or 80/12.

WOOL

Wool fabrics are excellent for sewing because they can be shaped easily, and they hold their shape well. Wool is available in every conceivable weave, texture, and finish. Because the fabric breathes, wool is comfortable to wear in all but extremely warm and humid weather.

Wool resists wrinkles, and contrary to popular belief, most woolens wash beautifully, although washing will change the appearance and hand of smoothly finished fabrics. Wool *must* be preshrunk before sewing if the finished product will be laundered. It should be washed in cool to tepid water as either extremely hot or extremely cold water will cause the fibers to mat and felt. It is best washed like silk, with soap, such as a livestock shampoo.

Gabardine is one of the best wool fabrics for clothing. It is light in weight, drapes attractively, and defies wrinkling. It can be challenging to press during construction: a damp pressing cloth, pounder, and point presser produce good results.

Challis is a very lightweight wool, suitable for tops, dresses, and soft skirts rather than structured garments. It is a pleasure to sew and, if preshrunk, washes very well.

Flannel has a napped finish and is a classic fabric for jackets and pants.

Crepe fabrics made of wool are beautiful to sew, and not difficult to press. Crepe can shrink even with dry cleaning, so have the cleaner steam the fabric before you cut it.

Synthetic and Man-made Fibers

Most fabrics made from synthetic fibers are easy to wash, and they resist wrinkling. Synthetic fibers are used for every kind of fabric weave and texture, and made to resemble natural fiber fabrics in appearance.

Most synthetic fabrics are quite stable—they don't tend to stretch out of shape. They also have little "ease," and cannot be shaped and molded as natural fiber fabrics can. Most synthetics are less expensive than their natural fiber counterparts, and are often blended with them to produce more economical fabrics.

Changes and improvements in synthetic fibers occur regularly and for this reason it is especially important with synthetic fabrics to follow manufacturers' guidelines for washing or dry cleaning and pressing. Some are sensitive to heat and will pucker or melt with the touch of a too-hot iron. Some will yellow if washed with chlorine bleach. Others are affected by certain chemicals: nail polish remover will dissolve acetate, for example.

Below are characteristics of some of the man-made fibers most widely available as yard goods.

ACETATE

Acetate is a crisp, fairly stiff fabric with considerable sheen. Unblended, it is used primarily for lining. It is often blended with cotton in faille and moire-patterned fabrics. It is prone to fading from sunlight, perspiration, and dry cleaning. Fabrics containing acetate should not be washed.

POLYESTER

The most widely used man-made fiber, polyester is extremely durable. It is available in every conceivable weave and texture. Polyester fabrics wash well, with little or no shrinkage, and dry quickly. They resent chlorine bleach, and too hot an iron may cause puckering or shrinking. They retain their shape, and they resist wrinkling and fading. The old varieties do not breathe well and can be uncomfortable to wear in temperatures of either extreme, but the new "breathable" polyester fabrics, the microfibers, are much better in this respect.

Polyester often is blended with natural fibers to give them strength and stability. The resulting blends often are less expensive and easier to care for than the comparable natural fiber fabrics, but they cannot be shaped and eased like their natural fiber counterparts, nor do they wear in the same graceful way.

Some of the lighter weight polyester fabrics, and the microfibers, will pucker when stitched. Try a shorter stitch length as a cure, and try one of the new needles designed for use with microfibers.

RAYON

Rayon is most appreciated for its draping qualities. It is somewhat of a hybrid, a man-made fiber that originates from a natural substance. Rayon, like acetate, is made of cellulose, but by a different process. The fabrics are not strong, and do not hold shape well, making them most suitable for fluid garment styles rather than structured ones. Rayon is often combined with fabrics which are stronger and more stable, such as cotton or polyester. Most rayons and rayon blends should be dry cleaned.

BLENDS

This is a confusing term. A blend of course can be any combination of fibers used to make up a fabric, such as cotton with ramie, or silk and wool. The term is most often used to indicate a mix of synthetic and natural fibers.

Fabrics for Linings

A lining should allow the garment to slip on easily, should have opacity in order to hide the garment's inner construction, and should be compatible with the outer garment fabric in terms of care requirements. Beyond that, anything goes.

A good traditional lining fabric for jackets is Bemberg rayon, which has some breathability and is reasonably priced. It should be dry cleaned.

Polyester lining fabrics are available in various grades. They are washable, but can be warm in summer weather.

Classic silk lining fabrics, China silk and habutae, are delicious to wear. They are somewhat more expensive than the synthetics.

Non-traditional linings can be fun to wear, as long as they meet the criteria. On a jacket, a luxurious piece of silk could be used to line the body, with a standard lining for the sleeves. The value of the garment would be doubled, while the increase in cost would be very slight.

Lining for a washable garment must be preshrunk along with the outer fabric.

Interfacings

Fabrics inside a garment, hidden from view once construction is completed, can affect the garment's appearance as much as the outer fabric does. Interfacing gives the garment its shape and provides support to areas like the collar, cuffs, and front edges.

There are an incredible number of interfacing materials available, and as new fabrics arrive on the scene, new interfacings are developed to back them up.

Interfacings are divided into two broad categories: fusible, or iron-on, and sew-in. They are also available in different weights, from featherweight to quite stiff. Following are descriptions of some basic types.

Woven interfacings may be all cotton, or a poly/cotton blend. They are quite stable, available in light to heavy weights. Wovens may be sew-in or fusible.

Hair canvas, Woven of wool, animal hair, and some synthetic fiber, is the ultimate interfacing for tailored garments. Synthetic versions are available in both fusible and sew-in versions.

Non-wovens are made of a fibrous material, and come in many forms and weights. Some are all-bias, meaning they stretch in all directions. They are available as fusibles or sew-in. With these interfacings particularly, don't stint on quality. The bargain varieties can shred after one or two washings, ruining a garment in which you've invested many hours.

Tricot knit interfacings are usually fusible, and available in featherweight or lightweight types. They are quite soft and stretchy, and are especially good with knits.

Weft insertion fusible interfacings also may be featherweight or lightweight. This is a knit/woven combination that is flexible, yet provides stability.

Cool-fuse, or *temporary bond* interfacings are hybrids. They press in place, but they don't actually bond to the fabric and must be sewed into the seams. They are woven rayon, extremely light in weight, and are well-suited to lightweight silks and sand washed silks.

Other fabrics which make excellent interfacing are cotton organdy, for medium to heavy cottons, and nylon chiffon, for lightweight fabrics which won't be subjected to a hot iron.

The interfacing question can be confusing to a novice sewer—it certainly is to the experienced ones! When you buy your fabric, ask for suggestions as to a compatible interfacing. Every fusible interfacing/fabric combination should be tested, and the sample washed if possible. Remember that any fusible interfacing will stiffen the fabric to some degree. Manufacturers' instructions should be followed to the letter.

Preparing the Fabrics

If you plan to wash your finished garment, all its component fabrics must be preshrunk before you sew. This simply means to wash the fabrics—lining and sew-in interfacing too—the way you plan to wash the garment. Even if your garment will be line dried, it's a good idea to dry the fabric in the drier just the one time. Then press the fabric, in the direction of the lengthwise grain. Don't press the center crease.

Cotton knit fabrics should be washed and machine dried at least twice to preshrink them.

Fabrics that will be dry cleaned, wools particularly, can be steamed to shrink them. Some wools, such as crepe, should be steamed by a dry cleaner before cutting.

Fusible interfacings also must be preshrunk, especially if they will be used for a washable garment. Most of them will shrink. The result is the same as imperfect bonding: an unsightly bubbled appearance to the garment.

Soak the interfacing for fifteen minutes or so in almost-hot water. Roll it in a towel, pressing gently. Then hang it to dry, smoothing out any wrinkles. Steam it then, holding the iron about an inch above the fabric surface.

Shirt with Convertible Collar

A truly great shirt pattern is the mainstay of a wardrobe that works. This basic shirt can very dressy or wonderfully casual, depending on the fabric used to make it. The pattern has unlimited potential for variation and experimentation. Wear an oversized version as a tunic over pants or a skirt; cut it smaller for a perfect all-occasion blouse. Add any sort of pocket, add trim, or embellish with decorative stitching—use your imagination and create your own special design.

The shirt is loose-fitting, with a collar that can be worn open or closed. The long sleeves have buttoned cuffs. Side seams have faced slits at the hem. Pockets with or without flaps can be added if desired.

INSTRUCTIONS

Detailed information about working with the patterns begins on page 106. For many of the construction steps, additional instructions are given in the Sewing Techniques section, page 111. The pattern is on page 118.

MATERIALS

Fabric

LONG-SLEEVED TOP WITH CUFFS

45" (115 cm) fabric:

    All sizes, 3 yds (2.75 m)

60" (152 cm) fabric:

    All sizes, 1-7/8 yds (1.75 m)

Lay out pattern pieces to determine fabric requirements for fabric of different widths than above, if substantial alterations are made, or if fabric pattern must be matched.

Other Materials

- Approximately 1 yd (.95 m) fusible or sew-in interfacing in a weight suitable for your fabric
- Buttons for front and cuffs
- Lightweight shoulder pads if desired

The soft, pretty rayon and cotton blend fabric of this blouse is comfortable and carefree, still fresh-looking at the end of a long day. Add another shirt over top, made from the solid-colored fabric used for the pants, to create an entirely different look.

The shirt in this photograph comes from Pattern A. For the pants, refer to Pattern G.

Add seam and hem allowances to all pieces before cutting.

Fold fabric in half lengthwise as shown and cut pieces 1, 2, 3, and two of piece 4. For faced slits at lower side seams, determine length of finished slit, with upper end approximately 3" (8 cm) below natural waistline. Along the slit, extend side seam allowances on front and back by the width of the hem allowance (1-1/2" or 4 cm is a good width for both), tapering extension to the width of the seam allowance above the upper end of the slit as shown below.

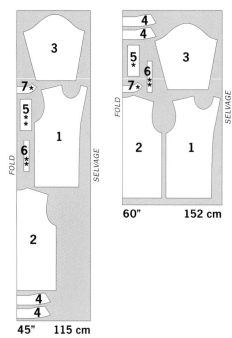

60" 152 cm

45" 115 cm

Pattern pieces

1. Front
2. Back
3. Sleeve
4. Collar
**5. Cuff
**6. Sleeve placket binding
*7. Back neck facing

* This piece is cut from another pattern piece as described in the cutting instructions.

** Pattern pieces not provided. Finished measurements are given with instructions; add seam/hem allowances before cutting. When multiple measurements are given, the first measurement is for the smallest size, followed by measurements for subsequently larger sizes.

Use piece 2 to cut piece 7. Cut two cuffs: 3" (8 cm) wide and 8-3/4", 9-1/8", 9-1/2", 9-7/8" (22, 23, 24, 25 cm) long. Cut two sleeve placket binding strips, 7" (17.5 cm) long and 1" (2.5 cm) wide. Cut breast pockets, if desired, from pocket pattern on page 141. Cut interfacing: two from self facing section of piece 1 and one for collar. For cuffs, cut interfacing the length of the cuff and half the width. Add seam allowances at outer edges for sew-in interfacing.

CONSTRUCTION

Fronts

1. Fuse interfacing to wrong side of front self facings following manufacturer's instructions. For sew-in interfacing, stitch to inner edge of facing section with right sides together. Turn; press. With fusible interfacing, turn under and press facing seam allowance on outer edge, stitch close to fold, then trim. Interface back neck facing in the same way.

2. Make pockets and stitch in place according to instructions on page 89.

3. Stitch back to fronts at shoulders.

Collar and facings

4. Staystitch neck edge and upper curved edges of self facings: stitch just outside the seamline in the seam allowance using a regular stitch length setting.

5. Fuse or baste interfacing to one collar section (the upper collar). With right sides together, stitch collar sections across ends and outer edge. Trim seam allowances and corners; turn and press. Baste neckline edges together.

6. Pin collar to neckline, with under collar to right side of shirt. Match at center back and front neckline points. Stitch, trim, and press. Edgestitch or topstitch outer edges.

7. With right sides together, stitch upper ends of front facings to ends of back neck facing. Trim and press.

8. Fold front facing sections wrong side out along the front foldlines. Stitch facing neck edges to shirt/collar, stitching just inside the collar seamline. Trim and press.

9. Understitch facings to keep them from rolling to the outside: Stitch fac-

ing to collar/neck seam allowances approximately 3/16" (.5 cm) from the neck seamline.

Sleeve plackets and cuffs

10. To reinforce upper end of sleeve placket, stitch outside the marked slash line with a short stitch, pivoting at the upper end of the placket. Slash to the upper point between stitching lines.

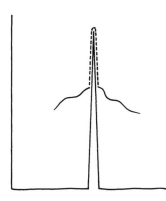

STITCH TO REINFORCE THE UPPER END OF THE PLACKET.

11. With right side of placket binding to wrong side of sleeve, stitch sleeve placket binding strip to placket. Keep 1/4" (7 mm) seam allowance on the binding strip but gradually decrease placket seam allowance to almost nothing just outside the reinforcing stitching at the placket upper end. Press seam allowances toward binding. Treat the upper end of the placket with a drop or two of liquid fray retardant. Turn binding to right side and fold in raw edge 1/4" (7 mm); press. Fold pressed edge over stitching; press and baste. Stitch very close to the binding edge, pivoting stitching at the upper end of the placket.

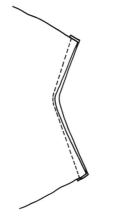

SEW BINDING TO PLACKET, STITCHING JUST OUTSIDE REINFORCING STITCHES AT PLACKET UPPER END.

12. Fold binding edges together; press. At the upper end, stitch both sides of the binding together from the pivot point diagonally to the binding edges.

STITCH ACROSS UPPER END OF PLACKET BINDING.

13. Turn front binding to inside; press, and baste across lower edge. Press back binding flat.

14. Fuse or baste interfacing to wrong side of each cuff, aligning or basting edge of interfacing at lengthwise center line of cuff.

15. Fold cuff in half lengthwise, right sides together. Stitch each end from folded edge to sleeve seamline. Turn; press.

16. Stitch lower 6" (15 cm) of sleeve seam and finish seam as desired.

17. Fold and press pleats at lower edge of sleeve and fit sleeve to cuff, adjusting pleats if necessary. Baste across pleats at the seamline.

18. With interfaced cuff section to right side of sleeve, stitch cuff to sleeve. Trim; press seam allowance toward cuff.

19. Fold in seam allowance on inner edge of cuff so that fold just covers cuff/sleeve stitching; press. Trim excess seam allowance. Pin or baste.

20. On right side, edgestitch cuff close to sleeve seamline, catching inner edge of cuff. Topstitch outer edges.

Sleeves and side seams

21. Ease stitch upper edges of sleeves. Loosen upper thread tension slightly, but use a normal stitch length. On right side, stitch along seamline of sleeve cap between front and back matching points.

22. Draw up bobbin thread of ease stitching and fit sleeve to armhole, matching underarm seamlines, shoulder, and matching points. Pin and stitch with right sides together. Trim and overcast seam allowances; press toward shirt.

With the addition of a snappy vest, this simple shirt and slacks become a nicely coordinated outfit. The vest is reversible, its lining the same silk and cotton blend fabric in green. The pants have slightly tapered legs with decorative slits at the hems. Add a jacket and slim skirt of solid periwinkle and you're set for a weekend anywhere!

For the blouse, refer to Pattern A, with short sleeves. The vest is from Pattern I, reversible variation. The pants are from Pattern G, with tapered legs.

Lightweight rayon and washable silk have the draping quality essential to the soft look of these elegant and comfortable separates. Perfect for a summer dinner party or day in the city, they are great traveling companions when teamed with the basic black pants and jacket.

The top ties in front at the waist, and has breast pockets with rounded lower corners. The pants are cut slightly wider in the hips, with side inseam pockets. Elastic at the waist makes them quick to construct.

For the blouse, refer to Pattern A, with short sleeves and tie front. The Pants are from Pattern G, elasticized waist and widened legs.

23. Stitch side and remainder of sleeve in a continuous seam, beginning at upper end of the side slit.

Hem and finishing

24. Fold under 1/2" (1.5 cm) on the side slit facings and hem. Press; stitch close to fold.

25. Press slit facings to inside along the seamlines. Press hem.

26. Miter the corners. Unfold the facing and hem at a corner and refold on the diagonal across the intersection of the creases as illustrated, matching the creases. Press this fold, then fold diagonal edges so they meet on the inside. Stitch the folds together by hand.

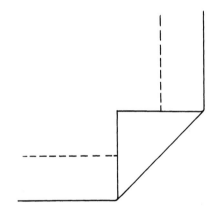

MITER THE CORNER WHERE HEM AND VENT FACING MEET.

27. Turn front facings to wrong side along foldlines, matching and stitching along pressed hemline. Trim; turn.

28. Stitch the hem by hand or machine. Reinforce across the upper end of each slit with a bar tack or a few machine zigzag stitches.

29. Topstitch front edges and across lower edges to hem stitching.

30. Mark buttonhole and button positions on front and cuffs. Sew buttons in place.

31. Stitch in shoulder pads, if desired.

Short sleeves

Copy the sleeve pattern piece and fold it across the marked line (or at the length desired). Make sure the fold line is exactly perpendicular to the lengthwise grain line.

Determine the amount of hem to be added—1-1/4" is standard, with 1/2" to turn under (3 cm and 1 cm). Trace the side seamlines of the hem so they match those of the sleeve. Cut across, keeping the cut line parallel to the hem.

Tie Front Variation

Enlarge the diagram to actual size by photocopying, or copy the new lines onto pattern drafting fabric printed with a 1" grid.

1. Alter the front pattern piece according to the diagram. The fold-line for the facing will become the facing seamline for this variation. The lower edge of the shirt should be 2" to 3" (5 cm to 8 cm) below the natural waistline to allow for blousing. Shorten the back pattern piece as shown. Check that side seamlines match in length. Add seam allowances before cutting.

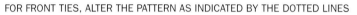

FOR FRONT TIES, ALTER THE PATTERN AS INDICATED BY THE DOTTED LINES

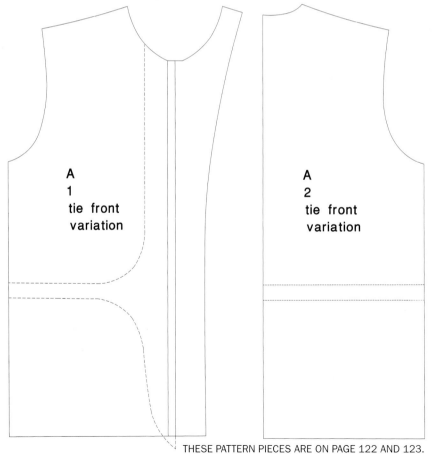

A
1
tie front
variation

A
2
tie front
variation

THESE PATTERN PIECES ARE ON PAGE 122 AND 123.

2. Use a very lightweight fabric to interface. Cut interfacing from the front facing pattern, ending it at the waistline.

3. Alter the sleeve pattern for the short-sleeved variation described above.

4. Stitch or fuse interfacing to front facings as described in step 1 of the basic shirt instructions.

5. Stitch back facing to lower edge of back with right sides together.

6. Complete steps 2 through 7 of the basic instructions.

7. With right sides together, pin facing to lower edges, ties, fronts, and neckline. Stitch, pivoting at upper front corners. Trim. Where possible, press seam allowances toward facing.

8. Understitch the collar area as described in step 9 of the general instructions.

9. Sew sleeves as described in steps 21 and 22 of the general instructions.

10. Stitch side seams, stitching back to front facings, sides, and sleeve in a continuous seam.

11. Turn facings to inside; press along seamline.

12. Edgestitch or topstitch upper fronts from collar, front edges, around ties and lower edge. On the inside tack facings at side seam allowances.

13. Mark buttonhole and button positions. Place the lowermost button slightly above the waistline so as not to interfere with tying the ties.

Add a Back Yoke

A yoke in back is a traditional detail and it allows you to make the lower back wider. Add a center pleat to fit the lower back to the yoke, and experiment with a decorative tab of your own design to sew above the pleat.

1. Copy the back pattern piece. Cut across the piece approximately 5-1/2" (14 cm) below the neckline and perpendicular to center back. Add seam allowance at both cut edges.

2. Cut the yoke with its straight edge on the lengthwise fabric grain.

3. To widen the lower back, place pattern center back 1-1/2" (4 cm) from the lengthwise fabric fold and parallel to it.

4. Cut the back, cutting upper edge straight across to the fabric fold. Mark center back.

5. Pleat the upper edge. On the right side, crease the fabric 3/4" (2 cm) from center and fold a pleat 3/4" (2 cm) deep. Fold another pleat at the other side of center so the inner pleat creases meet at center back.

6. Stitch yoke to lining with right sides together.

For a lined yoke, cut 2 yoke pieces as above. Substitute the yoke lining section for the back neck facing when constructing the shirt. After collar and yoke lining have been attached, turn under and baste lining seam allowances at shoulders and back yoke seam, just covering previous stitching. Edgestitch yoke on the right side.

Blouse with Straight Sleeves

For a sleeve without a cuff, narrow the pattern as shown and cut straight across the lower edge. Be sure it is wide enough for your hand to pass through easily.

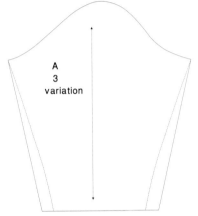

STRAIGHT SLEEVE VARIATION.
THIS PATTERN PIECE IS ON PAGE 121.

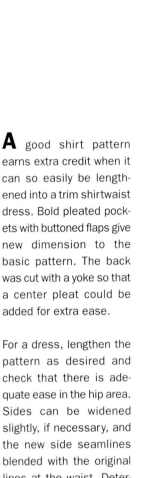

A good shirt pattern earns extra credit when it can so easily be lengthened into a trim shirtwaist dress. Bold pleated pockets with buttoned flaps give new dimension to the basic pattern. The back was cut with a yoke so that a center pleat could be added for extra ease.

For a dress, lengthen the pattern as desired and check that there is adequate ease in the hip area. Sides can be widened slightly, if necessary, and the new side seamlines blended with the original lines at the waist. Determine the waistline, allowing 1" to 2" (2.5 to 5 cm) ease for blousing above the belt. Stitch the back pleat at the waistline for neatness.

A very basic pattern looks anything *but* basic made up in three compatible silk crepe prints. It is a bright topper for the everyday black skirt or pair of pants, and would make a fabulous out-on-the-town dress worn with a full skirt in one of the prints. This blouse was cut slightly shorter than the pattern indicates so it will tuck comfortably into pants. For tips on working with lightweight silks, see page 15.

PATTERN
B

Collarless Tunic

Wonderfully versatile, this tunic pattern can be adapted for day or evening wear, made into a jacket, or lengthened into a beach dress. The basic version is quick and easy to make. Optional button loops (best attempted only with lightweight silky fabrics) on the front and sleeve plackets add a designer touch.

INSTRUCTIONS

Detailed information about working with the patterns is on page 106. For many of the construction steps, additional instructions are given in the Sewing Techniques section that begins on page 111. The pattern is on page 124.

MATERIALS

Fabric

LONG-SLEEVED TUNIC

45" (115 cm) fabric:
    Size XXS/XS, 2-1/2 yds (2.30 m)
    Size L/XL, 2-3/4 yds (2.55 m)

60" (152 cm) fabric:
    Sizes XXS/XS, 1-7/8 yds (1.75 m)
    Sizes L/XL, 2 yds (1.85 m)

Lay out pattern pieces to determine fabric requirements for fabric of different widths, if substantial alterations are made, or if fabric pattern must be matched.

Other Materials

- Approximately 1 yard (.95 m) interfacing of a type and weight suited to your fabric
- Buttons for front and sleeve plackets
- Lightweight shoulder pads if desired

CUTTING

Add seam and hem allowances to all pieces before cutting.

Fold fabric in half lengthwise and cut pieces 1, 2, and 3. Cut piece 4 using pattern piece 1, and piece 5 using pattern piece 2.

Cut two sleeve placket binding strips 8" (20 cm) long and 1-3/4" (4 cm) wide.

For each button loop, measure the circumference of the button and add 1/2" (1 cm) for seam allowances. Multiply by the number of buttons for total length needed, and add a little extra. Cut this piece 1" (2 cm) wide on the bias from a single thickness of fabric. Cut as a single length if possible.

If you are using button loops, place the right front against the pattern piece again and mark the center front. Add seam allowance, then cut away excess along the front. (Right front facing seamline is the center front line.) Trim the same amount from the right front facing piece.

To make the blouse with standard buttonholes, cut the right front the same as the left front and work buttonholes after construction is finished.

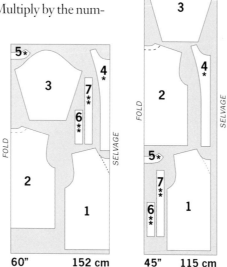

Pattern pieces
1. Front
2. Back
3. Sleeve
*4. Front facing
*5. Back neck facing
**6. Sleeve placket binding
**7. Button loop strip

*This piece is cut from another pattern piece as described in the cutting instructions.
**Pattern pieces not provided. Finished measurements are given with instructions; add seam/hem allowances before cutting. When multiple measurements are given, the first measurement is for the smallest size, followed by measurements for subsequently larger sizes.

CONSTRUCTION

Button loops

1. Fold the button loop strip(s) in half lengthwise, wrong side out. Stitch long edges together with a 1/4" (.5 cm) seam allowance.

2. Trim away half the seam allowances. Turn right side out with a loop turner. If you don't have this tool, thread a strong needle with several strands of thread somewhat longer than the piece. Knot the threads together at one end and take several stitches through the seam allowance and stitching line close to one end of the tube. Back the needle through the tube to pull it right side out.

Cut the loop strip into individual lengths.

Facings and neckline

3. Fuse interfacing to wrong side of front facings following manufacturer's instructions. For sew-in interfacing, stitch to inner edge of facing section with right sides together. Turn; press. With fusible interfacing, turn under and press facing seam allowance on outer edge, stitch close to fold, then trim. Interface back neck facing in the same way. Stitch back neck facing to upper ends of front facings with right sides together.

4. Stitch back to fronts at shoulders with right sides together.

5. Staystitch neckline of blouse by stitching just inside the seamline with a regular length stitch.

6. Position button loops on right side of right front, ends close together and aligned with front edge.

7. With right sides together, pin facing to blouse along front edges and around neckline.

8. Stitch. Trim corners and press seam allowances toward facings. Understitch

The tunic in soft sand-washed silk is magnificent over pants or a long straight skirt. For a less formal look it can be worn unbuttoned over a tank top of the same silk or lightweight knit.

Construct the tunic following the basic instructions, using the pattern's V-neckline. Read the tips on sewing with lightweight silks, page 15, if you haven't yet worked with this luxurious fabric. Try a cool-fuse interfacing to stabilize the fabric without adding stiffness.

Create a perfect suit for the contradictory weather of late spring when you long for softer colors but still appreciate the warmth of wool. Both the jacket and blouse are made from the tunic pattern, the jacket and pants in lightweight wool crepe and the blouse in silk crepe. For an elegant touch, line the jacket with the same silk used for the blouse.

The jacket sports lined and buttoned patch pockets, smaller ones above and larger ones below, their check pattern perfectly matched to the jacket front. The jacket shown is cut approximately 2" (6 cm) longer than the pattern. The sleeves do not have placket openings. Instructions for the jacket variation are on page 31.

Make the blouse according to the basic instructions too, omitting the sleeve plackets. To make it very special, add silk-covered buttons as shown. Line the covering fabric for better opacity. The pants are made with Pattern G.

facings to keep them from rolling to the outside: Stitch facing to collar/neck seam allowances approximately 3/16" (.5 cm) from the neck seamline. If top-stitching will be worked later under-stitching is not necessary.

Sleeves

9. To reinforce upper end of sleeve placket, stitch outside the marked slash line with a short stitch, pivoting at the upper end of the placket. Cut to the upper point between stitching lines.

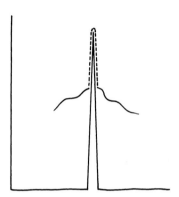

STITCH TO REINFORCE THE UPPER END OF THE PLACKET.

10. Position the desired number of button loops on the front edge of the sleeve placket, on the right side. Place one loop approximately 3/4" (2 cm) from the upper end of the placket, another 1/2" (1 cm) from the hem-line, and space the others evenly between. Pin in place, ends close together and aligned with the placket edge. Baste.

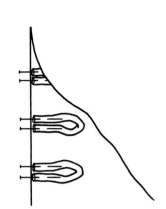

ON THE RIGHT SIDE, POSITION BUTTON LOOPS ALONG THE FRONT PLACKET OPENING.

11. With right sides together, stitch sleeve placket binding strip to plack-et. Keep 1/4" (7 mm) seam allowance on the binding strip but gradually decrease placket seam allowance from 1/2" (1 cm) at the sleeve lower edge to almost nothing just outside the rein-forcing stitching at the placket upper end. Press seam allowances toward binding. Apply a drop or two of liquid fray retardant to the seam allowance at the upper end of the placket. Fold binding raw edge 1/4" (7 mm) to wrong side; press.

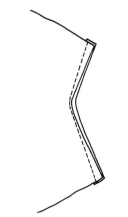

SEW BINDING TO PLACKET, STITCHING JUST OUTSIDE REINFORCING STITCHES AT PLACKET UPPER END.

12. Fold binding to inside so folded edge just covers stitching line. Hand stitch in place.

13. Fold binding edges together; press. At the upper end, stitch both sides of the binding together from the pivot point diagonally to the binding edges.

STITCH ACROSS UPPER END OF PLACKET BINDING.

14. Turn front binding to inside; press. Press back binding flat.

15. Ease stitch upper edges of sleeves: Loosen upper thread tension slightly, but use a normal stitch length. On right side, stitch along seamline of sleeve cap between front and back matching points.

16. Draw up bobbin thread of ease stitching and fit sleeve to armhole, matching underarms, shoulder, and matching points. Pin and stitch with right sides together. Trim and overcast seam allowances; press toward blouse.

Side seams and finishing

17. Pin back to front at sides, and pin sleeve back to front. Stitch in a con-tinuous seam. Press, and finish seam as desired.

18. At lower edges of each sleeve, open out front binding and press hem in place. Stitch hem by hand or machine. Re-fold front binding over hem and hand stitch binding edge to hem.

19. Fold and press hem at lower edge of blouse and facings. Turn front facings to wrong side along front seamlines, matching and stitching along pressed hemline. Trim; turn right side out.

20. Stitch the hem by hand or machine.

21. Tack facings loosely at shoulder seams. Stitch shoulder pads in place if desired.

22. Mark button positions on left front and sleeves. Sew on buttons.

Jacket Variation

In addition to the jacket fabric, you will need lining fabric, fusible or sew-in interfacing compatible with the outer fabric for the facings, and lightweight sew-in interfacing for the sleeve and lower hems. You will also need buttons for the front and pockets, and shoulder pads.

Pattern adjustments and cutting

1. Widen front facing by approximately 1" (1.5 cm) along the front edge, tapering to the original seamline at shoulder.

2. Make a lining pattern according to the instructions on page 114.

3. Cut the jacket according to the instructions for the tunic, adding seam allowances and 1-1/2" (4 cm) hem allowances on front, back, and sleeves. Add seam allowance.

4. Cut lining, following the instructions on page 114.

5. Cut fusible or sew-in interfacing for facing pieces.

6. Cut bias strips of the lightweight sew-in interfacing for hems. Cut these 2-1/2" (6.5 cm) wide, two the length of the sleeve lower edge and one the length of the combined back and front lower edges.

CONSTRUCTION

Front, back, and facings

7. Baste sew-in interfacing to wrong side of front facing pieces along shoulder, neckline, front, and lower edges, stitching in the seam allowance just outside the seamline. Baste to shoulder and neckline edges of back neck facing in the same way. Trim away excess seam allowance. Stitch facing and interfacing together along outer edges of all pieces with a zigzag or overcast stitch. Stitch front facings to back neck facing at shoulders with right sides together.

8. Make lined patch pockets according to the instructions on page 91. Work buttonholes at the upper center of each pocket. Baste pockets to the jacket fronts, then topstitch in place. Sew on buttons, using a small piece of interfacing to reinforce behind each one.

9. With right sides together, stitch jacket front sections to back at shoulders.

10. Staystitch jacket neck edge, stitching 3/16" (.5cm) outside the seamline in the seam allowance. Pin facing to jacket, right sides together, along fronts and around neckline. Stitch; trim and grade seam allowances. Press seam allowances toward facing, then press facings toward inside along seam.

Sleeves and side seams

11. Ease stitch upper edges of sleeves: Loosen upper thread tension slightly, and use a normal stitch length. On right side, stitch along seamline of sleeve cap between front and back matching points.

12. Pin sleeve to jacket, right sides together, matching marks and easing fullness. Stitch. Trim and overcast seam allowances; press toward sleeve.

13. Pin side seam and sleeve; stitch as one continuous seam.

14. Position and stitch shoulder pads.

Hems

15. Pin hem at jacket lower edge; press lightly.

16. Fold front facings to wrong side along seamline. Match and stitch to front along hemline. Trim; turn and press.

17. Open out hem. Position longer bias interfacing strip along hem, upper edge of the the strip 2" (5 cm) above hemline and lower edge folded into the hemline. Trim off ends of strip just inside front facings. Catchstitch invisibly to jacket as shown. Re-fold jacket hem; press. Stitch by hand to the interfacing.

The tunic is paired with a long, graceful skirt for that one dress every wardrobe needs. Made of silk noil, washed first for softness, it is comfortable to wear almost year round and just right for almost any occasion. Buttons and button loops are sewn in triplets for a clever design variation that's easy to accomplish.

The skirt, from Pattern D, has a trio of buttons and loops at the back vent. The overlay side of the vent has a separate facing to provide a seam into which button loops can be sewn.

Buy the fabric in the morning and wear it to tonight's party? Every sewer has done it – sometimes with less than spectacular results. The secret is a good basic pattern that adapts readily to any sort of fabric. The tunic here is made up in metallic fabric that's definitely party minded. In the interest of quick construction, standard buttonholes are used on the front (a fabric like this one needs little in the way of embellishment) and sleeve vents were omitted. Topstitching around fronts and lower edge provides a finishing touch. Underneath is a simple long-sleeved shirt, made from Pattern C with the neckline lowered slightly.

Metallic fabrics require a little special handling. Since metal can dull tools, use an old pair of shears to cut it. If the fabric ravels badly use liquid fray retardant on the edges, as overstitching these fabrics can stretch them out of shape. Use a basting spray or tape instead of pins wherever possible. Try a sharp machine needle instead of one with a universal point, a "jeans" needle or one designed for use with microfibers, and replace it once or twice during the course of the project if necessary.

Test any substance on a scrap before using it on a visible area of the garment to be sure it won't discolor the fabric. Test pressing techniques, too: Heat can damage some metallic fabrics, and many need only finger pressing or pressure from a clapper to flatten the seams.

The blouse under this Pattern B tunic is a T-shirt from Pattern C, with the neckline dramatically lowered. If a perfectly matched ensemble is your wardrobe staple, you will come back to Pattern C again and again.

CATCHSTITCH HEM INTERFACING TO JACKET.

18. Hem sleeves in the same way.

Lining

19. Fold a 1/2" (1.5 cm) pleat at each side of center back so pleats meet at center. Press, and baste at the seamline.

20. Stitch fronts to back at shoulders, right sides together. Staystitch neckline as for jacket.

21. Ease stitch and set in sleeves as for the jacket.

22. Stitch side and sleeve seams.

23. With right sides together, pin and stitch lining to jacket front and neck facings, beginning and ending seam approximately 6" (15 cm) above lower edge.

24. Along the lower edge, match lining edge to edge of jacket hem (a pleat will form). Stitch by hand 1/2" (1.5 cm) below raw edges, easing full-

ness across back. Hand stitch remainder of lining/facing seams at lower edges. Stitch lower ends of facing to jacket hem.

25. Hand stitch lining to sleeve hems in the same way.

Finishing

26. Topstitch front and neck edges, ending stitching at facing edges on lower front.

27. Mark and stitch buttonholes. Sew on buttons.

Sewing with Knits

Clothes made of knitted fabrics are a pleasure to wear. They are comfortable, and they are undemanding about upkeep. The advantage to making your own knitwear is that you can make sure you don't end up with an elbow-length shirt or knee-length pants unless you plan them that way. Knits are not at all difficult to sew, but do require some special treatment.

KNIT FABRICS

Knits are manufactured as "single" and "double" fabrics. A single knit is constructed in much the same way as a hand-knitted sweater, with a different look to the face and reverse sides. Double knits are the same on both sides. These are usually more stable and lack the tendency to curl toward the right side, an aggravation for the sewer. Look for quality when buying knit fabric. Bargain knits often have a built-in torque that cannot be straightened, and are more likely to curl at the cut edges.

Knit fabric can be made of almost any fiber. The fabric will exhibit the characteristics of the fiber as well as of the knit construction. Cotton or cotton/polyester blends are widely available, and are probably the easiest to work with and the nicest to wear. Luxurious silk and rayon knits are a little trickier to sew and usually must be dry cleaned. Wool double knits make into reliable, long-wearing garments. Polyester double knits. . . well, yes, they're still around.

Knit garments usually need interfacing only under facings and behind buttons and buttonholes. Choose an interfacing designed for knits. Fusible tricot, for one, has the necessary amount of stretch and it won't stiffen the fabric.

The best pattern choice for a knit is a simple garment with straight lines and few, if any, cross-grain seams. To make a test garment for a pattern to be used for knit fabric, use another knit. Woven fabric does not perform in the same way and won't give an accurate idea of the garment.

PREPARING TO SEW

Don't for a minute consider cutting into a cotton or cotton blend knit without first preshrinking it. Even a good quality fabric can shrink as much as 20 percent in length. Knits should be washed and machine dried at least twice before cutting even if the garment itself will never see the inside of a dryer. Three times is safer still. It is a good idea to buy a little extra fabric and be prepared for some shrinkage.

Take time to smooth the fabric carefully on a table before cutting. A grid-printed cardboard cutting mat is very useful for squaring the fabric. Re-fold the fabric to avoid the manufacturer's center crease—it's usually permanent.

Garment pieces can be cut most accurately with a rotary cutter. This eliminates the need to pin pattern to fabric, which can stretch the piece out of shape.

SEWING KNITS

The greatest aid to sewing knits is the serger. It stitches, trims, and overcasts a seam in a single pass through the machine. A serger usually will not stretch the seamline of a knit fabric as a conventional sewing machine can do. Newer models are equipped with an adjustable feed mechanism to deal with even the stretchiest fabrics. For most knits, a three-thread set-up will produce a seam with the correct amount of stretch.

SELECTING THE BEST STITCH

Stitches used on knits must stretch as the fabric does, or seams will pucker and thread will break. Any stitch in which the needle moves from side to side will work. About the only stitch that won't do is an ordinary straight stitch. When the seams calls for a straight stitch, at the neck facing for example, a very narrow zigzag stitch produces a seam that stretches slightly yet looks like a straight stitched seam on the outside.

Many machines have built-in knit stitches that sew a seam and overcast edges at the same time. Many of these are overrated. Since most knits don't ravel, the seam allowances don't

Sewing with Knits

require much in the way of finishing. Knits fare better with fewer stitches worked into them—heavy stitching only stretches the fabric. With many of these stitches it is best to use a standard seam allowance of 1/2" to 5/8" (1.5 cm) then trim away the excess. Stitching right at the fabric edge can result in a wavy seam.

Seams sewn across the grain are most likely to ripple, as the fabric stretches most in that direction. For cross-grain seams, or hems, stitch well away from the fabric edge. If your pattern has crossgrain seams, cut a wider seam allowance for these, and trim after stitching. Sew machine-stitched hems the same way. To prevent cross-grain seams from stretching out of shape, at the shoulders and back of the neck for example, stitch a tape stay into the seamline. Stabilizing tape is available for this purpose or, in an emergency, the selvage cut from a piece of polyester lining fabric will do the job.

TOPSTITCHING

Some machines have a straight stitch designed for knits that is just right for topstitching. A decorative stitch can be attractive for topstitching too. Choose one that involves a side-to-side needle motion. Avoid the dense satin stitches, which will stretch the fabric.

A double needle—be sure it's a ballpoint—is excellent for topstitching. It sews a double line of straight stitch on the front with a zigzag stitch on the reverse side, so that the resulting line of stitching has enough stretch for the knit.

BUTTONHOLES AND BUTTONS

It is especially important to interface behind buttons and buttonholes on knits. The stitching of a buttonhole is quite dense and it will most likely ripple without interfacing to support it. If the garment interfacing is very light, add a small piece of sturdier interfacing or tear-away backing behind each buttonhole then trim away the excess. If your machine permits, lengthen the stitch for the buttonholes, too, to lessen the density of the stitching.

Corded buttonholes are ideal for knits. Most buttonhole feet are capable of making them, and instructions should be given in your machine manual.

TIPS FOR SEWING KNITS

- Always use a ballpoint needle. A sharp or universal point will cut threads of the fabric and cause holes or runs.

- Use polyester thread. It has slightly more stretch than cotton-wrapped polyester, and considerably more than cotton.

- During construction, pin on a flat surface to avoid stretching the garment pieces.

- If fabric stretches during sewing and the seam ripples, try pushing the fabric toward the needle so there is always a slight hump just in front of the presser foot. Never pull the fabric from behind the needle.

- If fabric layers feed unevenly during stitching, use a Teflon foot or roller foot, or best, a walking or even-feed foot. With a standard presser foot, loosen the pressure slightly if your machine has this capability.

Add the doubled collar, and add warmth and style to a plain T-shirt. The cardigan provides an interesting pattern mix and another cozy layer. It's made with Pattern B.

PATTERN

C

Sewing with Knits

T-shirt

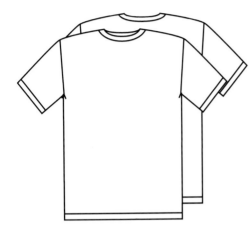

The simple T-shirt pattern has limitless wardrobe potential. Make it with long sleeves or short. Stitch a crew neck, a lowered neck, or a V. Add a placket opening, or a relaxed turtleneck collar. Collect a drawer full of them in comfortable cotton knit, then try the pattern with other soft fabrics too.

INSTRUCTIONS

Knit fabrics call for some special sewing techniques, described on the preceding pages. Detailed information about using the patterns is on page 106. The pattern is on page 126.

MATERIALS

Fabric:

SHORT-SLEEVED SHIRT

60" (152 cm) fabric:

All sizes, 1-3/8 yds (1.3 m)

LONG-SLEEVED SHIRT

Size XXS/XS, 1-5/8 yds (1.5 m)

Size L/XL, 1-3/4 yds (1.6 m)

Purchase extra fabric to allow for shrinkage.

Lay out pattern pieces to determine fabric requirements for fabric of a different width, if substantial alterations are made, or if fabric has a pattern that must be matched.

Other Materials

- Fusible knit interfacing, approximately 1/4 yd (.25 m)
- Stabilizing tape

CUTTING

Add seam and hem allowances to all pieces before cutting. It is not necessary to add seam allowance at neck facing outer edges. Fold fabric as shown and cut pieces 1, 2, 4, and 5 on lengthwise folds of the fabric. Piece 4 is cut from pattern piece 1; piece 5 from pattern piece 2. Cut piece 3 from doubled fabric. Cut interfacing for back and front neck facings without seam allowances.

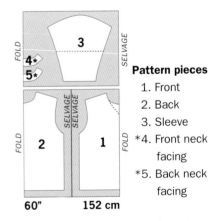

Pattern pieces

1. Front
2. Back
3. Sleeve
*4. Front neck facing
*5. Back neck facing

*These pieces are cut from other pattern pieces as described in the cutting nstructions.

CONSTRUCTION

1. Fuse interfacing to wrong sides of neck facings according to manufacturer's instructions. With right sides together, sew facings together at ends.

2. With right sides together, sew back to front at shoulders. For the V-neck, first stitch along the seamline at the front vee to reinforce. To prevent shoulder seams from stretching, cut two strips of stabilizing tape the length of the pattern shoulder seamline and incorporate a strip into each seam, easing the fabric to the tape.

3. Pin and stitch facing to neckline with right sides together, matching centers and shoulders. Trim, turn, and press lightly. Understitch facings by stitching facing to seam allowances 3/16" (.5 cm) from neckline seam, or topstitch.

4. Ease stitch upper edges of sleeves. Loosen upper thread tension slightly, but use a normal stitch length. On right side, stitch along seamline of sleeve cap between front and back matching points.

5. Draw up bobbin thread of ease stitching slightly to fit sleeve to armhole, matching underarm seams, shoulder, and matching points. Pin and stitch with right sides together. Trim.

6. Stitch side and sleeve in a continuous seam.

7. Fold and press hem at lower edge. Stitch with a hand or machine blind hem. As an alternative, stitch on the right side with a double needle or decorative stitch. Stitch 3/4" (2 cm) or more from the raw edge, then trim away excess.

Shirt with Buttoned Placket

The front placket is faced, and trimmed with a single button and loop buttonhole.

1. Determine placket length (on the shirt shown it is 2" or 5 cm). Lengthen front facing so it is 1" (2.5 cm) longer than placket, tapering to the original seamline at shoulder.

2. Fuse interfacing to the facings as for the shirt above, and fuse a strip 1" (2.5 cm) wide and 1/2" (1.5 cm) longer than the placket to the center front of the shirt at the placket location.

3. Join facings and stitch shoulders of shirt according to steps 1 and 2 above.

4. Mark placket with a straight line at center front of shirt and facing on the wrong sides. On shirt, reinforce around lower end of placket with short straight stitching, as shown.

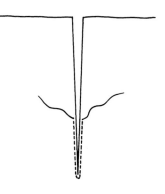

STITCH TO REINFORCE LOWER END OF SHIRT PLACKET BEFORE CUTTING.

5. Cut placket on shirt and on facing.

6. Make a button loop. Cut a strip of fabric as long as the button circumference, plus 1/2" (1 cm), and 1" (2.5 cm) wide. Stitch long edges with right sides together, using 1/4" (.5 cm) seam allowance. Trim seam allowance and turn. Baste to shirt right side, on right side of placket, 1/2" (1.5cm) below neck seamline with ends of loop at placket raw edge.

7. Pin facing to shirt, right sides together, carefully matching plackets. Stitch from shirt side. Pivot stitching at neck seamline 1/4" (.5 cm) from placket edges. Taper stitching line along placket to just outside reinforcing stitching at lower end. Trim and clip seam. Place a drop or two of fray retardant on the seam allowance at the placket lower end if desired. Turn and press lightly. Stitch the button in place.

8. Hem the shirt according to the basic shirt instructions above.

Shirt with Turtleneck Collar

This shirt variation is made like the basic shirt, but with a relaxed collar instead of neck facings. Lay out pattern pieces to determine yardage requirements.

1. Follow cutting instructions for the basic T-shirt, omitting the facings.

2. Make a pattern for the collar, 12-1/2" (32 cm) long, and in width 20-1/4" (51.5 cm) for size XXS/XS, and 21", 21-3/4", 22-3/4" (53.5, 55.5, 57.5 cm), for the subsequently larger sizes. Fold fabric lengthwise and cut one, pattern length on the fold, adding seam allowances.

3. With right sides together, sew shirt back to front at shoulders. To prevent

shoulder seams from stretching, cut two strips of stabilizing tape the length of the pattern shoulder seamline and incorporate a strip into each seam, easing the fabric to the tape.

4. With right sides together, stitch the collar long edges together to form a tube. Turn right side out. Fold in half and baste raw edges together.

5. Divide shirt neck edge into quarters: mark center front and back; mark halfway between. Mark collar raw edge in the same way, placing seam at center back.

6. Stitch collar to neck edge with right sides together.

7. Ease stitch upper edges of sleeves. Loosen upper thread tension slightly, but use a normal stitch length. On right side, stitch along seamline of sleeve cap between front and back matching points.

8. Draw up bobbin thread of ease stitching slightly to fit sleeve to armhole, matching underarm seamlines, shoulder, and matching points. Pin and stitch with right sides together. Trim.

7. Stitch side and sleeve in a continuous seam.

8. Fold and press hem at lower edge. Stitch with a hand or machine blind hem. As an alternative, stitch on the right side with a double needle or decorative stitch. Stitch 3/4" (2 cm) or more from the raw edge, then trim to stitching.

What could be more comfortable? Soft cotton jersey makes up beautifully in this T-shirt variation. The sleeves are shortened to three-quarter length, the neckline lowered slightly, and a small buttoned placket added for interest.

The pants were made from Pattern G, with an easy-to-wear elasticized waist. The vest is Pattern J, lengthened slightly and lined in the ocean blue of the pants and shirt. For this vest the armholes were tapered inward slightly at the shoulders.

These knit coordinates are comfortable enough to add to the pleasure of a leisurely Saturday breakfast, yet perfectly appropriate for tending to the day's errands later.

The leggings and cardigan are medium weight cotton double knit. Make the cardigan from Pattern B, eliminating the sleeve plackets. Pearly snap fasteners down the front are quicker to do than buttons and buttonholes. Be sure to interface behind them! Here the hems and topstitching are sewn with the machine's knit straight stitch, but a simple decorative stitch could be used instead.

Leggings with Elasticized Waist

This pattern is sized for stretchable knit fabrics. For use with a woven fabric it may be necessary to use the next size larger and/or to widen the lower leg slightly as described with the Pattern G variation for wider legs and elasticized waist, page 65.

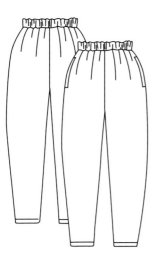

Sewing with Knits

INSTRUCTIONS

Knit fabrics call for some special sewing techniques, described in Sewing with Knits, page 37. Detailed information about using the patterns is on page 106. The pattern is on page 132.

MATERIALS

Fabric:

60" (152 cm):

Size XXS/XS, 1-3/8 yds (1.3 m)

Size L/XL, 1-7/8 yds (1.75 m)

Less yardage will be needed for the larger sizes if fabric is wider. Purchase extra fabric to allow for shrinkage. Lay out pattern pieces to determine fabric requirements for fabric of a different width, if substantial alterations are made, or if fabric has a pattern that must be matched.

Other Materials

- Waistband elastic, according to your measurement
- Lining fabric, 3/8 yd (.35 m), for pockets

CUTTING

Fold fabric on lengthwise grain and cut pieces as shown. Add seam and hem allowances before cutting. If inseam pockets will be added, see page 91 for cutting instructions. Waistband facing allows for an elastic casing. Be sure it is slightly wider than the elastic you plan to use, and add a narrow seam allowance at the upper edge. For flat-sewn waistband elastic, measure up from the waistline by the width of the elastic, add approximately 1/4" (.5 cm) ease, and add a seam allowance to turn under at the top. Cut elastic to waistline measurement plus 1" (2 cm).

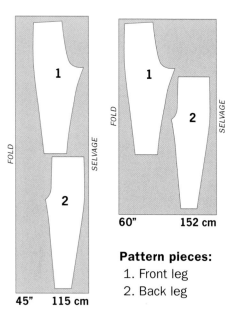

Pattern pieces:

1. Front leg
2. Back leg

CONSTRUCTION

1. To add pockets, follow the instructions on page 91.

2. With right sides together, stitch backs to fronts along outer side seams and inner leg seams.

3. Place one leg, right side out, inside the other leg (wrong side out) and stitch the crotch from the front upper edge to the back facing line for conventional elastic, or stop several inches below the back waistline for flat-sewn elastic.

4. For flat-sewn elastic, pin strip in place on wrong side, aligning lower edge with waistline. Turn upper edge under the strip. Stitch in place. Draw up elastic to fit waistline and stitch securely over ends in back seam allowances. Stitch remainder of back seam.

5. To create a casing for conventional elastic, fold to the inside along the facing line, folding under the seam allowances of the opening at the center back seam. On the outside, stitch 1-1/4" from the fold. Thread elastic through casing. Pull out both ends, overlap them 1/2" (1 cm) and stitch securely together. Arrange them in the casing and stitch the open center back seam.

6. Fold leg hems to wrong side, press, and stitch.

Straight Skirt

Make a short one, make a long one, and one strictly middle-of-the-road for days you don't feel like committing yourself.

This very slim skirt has front and back darts, and a faced vent in back. It can button up the front, or have a one-piece front with a back zipper. Side seam pockets can be added if desired. It acquires a wrap-around look with the over-lapping front panel added.

Almost any medium to fairly heavy fabric is suitable: cotton, wool, such as gabardine or flannel, heavier silks or linen.

INSTRUCTIONS

If you haven't made a test garment from the pattern (or made it a long time ago), it's wise to make the waistband first. Then baste the skirt darts, fit skirt to band, and adjust the darts if necessary.

Before cutting, determine finished skirt length; allow 1-1/2" (4 cm) or as desired for hem. Determine uppermost point of back vent—it should be 2" to 3" (5 cm to 8 cm) above the knee for walking ease. Adjust length of back vent facing extensions if necessary.

The pattern is on page 128.

A full range of autumn colors greets the season in grand style. All in cotton corduroy, these pieces are easy to wear together and to mix with other favorites.

The skirt, made from Pattern D, is lined to prevent clinging and to help the soft corduroy keep its shape.

The jacket, unlined and quick to make, comes from shirt Pattern A (instructions begin on page 18). The sleeves are cut straight across the bottom, with cuffs added for interest. Big patch pockets serve as handwarmers and hold the essentials—they're lined for durability. You might like to cut the shirt pattern half a size larger to wear over layers, especially when the fabric is bulky.

The shortened lined vest accents the skirt's length. To shorten the vest, just fold a pleat at the waistline of the pattern front and back, keeping it exactly perpendicular to the lengthwise grain lines. Smooth out the side seamlines and make sure they are the same length front and back. Instructions for Vest I begin on page 74.

MATERIALS

Fabric

LONG SKIRT, PLAIN FRONT WITH BACK ZIPPER

45" (115 cm):

> All sizes, 2-1/4 yds (2.10 m)

60" (152 cm):

> All sizes, 1-1/4 yds (1.15 m)

SHORT SKIRT, PLAIN FRONT, BACK ZIPPER

45" (115 cm):

> All sizes, 1-1/2 yds (1.40 m)

60" (152 cm):

> All sizes, 3/4 yd (.70 m)

LONG SKIRT, BUTTON FRONT

45" (115 cm):

> All sizes, 2-1/4 yds (2.10 m)

60" (152 cm):

> All sizes, 1-3/8 yds (1.30 m)

WITH FRONT PANEL

45" (115 cm):

> Size S, 2-1/4 yds (2.10 m)
>
> Size XL, 2-3/8 yds (2.20 m)

60" (152 cm):

> All sizes, 1-3/8 yds (1.30 m)

Lay out pattern pieces to determine fabric requirements for sizes and fabric widths not given above, if substantial alterations are made, or if fabric pattern must be matched.

Other Materials

- Waistband interfacing
- Zipper, 7" or 9" (18 cm or 22 cm)
- Waistband hook and eye for the straight or panel variation
- Buttons for the button front design

Straight Skirt
with Plain Front and Back Vent

CUTTING

Cut left back, adding hem allowance at outer vent facing hemline. Cut right back, adding hem allowance at inner vent facing hemline. Mark center back lines on vent extensions.

For waistband length, add to waist measurement 1" to 1-1/2" (2 cm to 4 cm) ease, plus 1-1/4" (3 cm) for underlay at center back, plus seam allowance at both ends. In width, allow for a finished width of 1-1/4" (3 cm), and cut the band 2-1/2" (6 cm) plus seam allowance at both sides. Cut from doubled fabric, with band center on lengthwise fabric fold as shown in the layout. For fabrics with considerable cross-grain stretch, cut band on lengthwise grain.

Cut fusible interfacing to the band finished width and length. Or use firm sew-in interfacing, cut to band finished length plus underlay and seam allowance, and to the finished width plus seam allowance on one long edge. For purchased waistband stay, follow manufacturer's instructions.

Cut front with center front line on lengthwise fold of fabric.

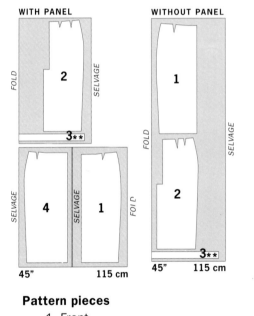

Pattern pieces

1. Front
2. Back
   **3. Waistband
3. Panel

** Pattern piece not provided. Finished measurements are given with instructions; add seam/hem allowances before cutting.

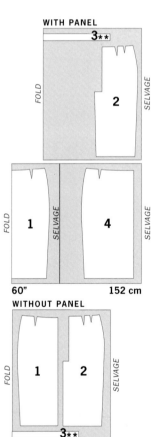

CONSTRUCTION

For some of the construction steps below, additional instructions are given in the Sewing Techniques section that begins on page 111.

Front and back

1. Stitch darts in front and back pieces.

2. To add side seam pockets, follow the instructions beginning on page 91.

3. On center back seamline, mark placement point for zipper lower end. Allow 1/4" (1 cm) between top zipper teeth and waist seamline. Mark upper end of back vent. Stitch seam between two marked points and baste upper end of the seam. Press open.

Zipper

4. Open zipper and place face down on wrong side of skirt back. Baste one side of zipper to seam allowance, aligning the teeth with the seamline.

5. With zipper foot, stitch along raised thread in zipper tape. Close the zipper. Baste the other side of the tape through all thicknesses.

6. Topstitch on the right side, beginning even with the marked point below the zipper stop and stitching 1/2" to 3/8" (7 mm to 1 cm) from the seamline. Stitch across the lower end and up the other side.

Vent

7. Clean finish edges of vent facing hems. Fold and press along hem lines; stitch close to folds.

8. Fold vent on skirt right to inside along center back line; press. Align fold with center back line on left skirt. Baste 6" (15 cm) or so from top of vent along fold.

9. On outside, stitch across upper vent facing seam allowances from top of vent to facing edges.

Sides and waistband

If belt loops will be added, see instructions on page 112.

10. With right sides together, stitch back to front at side seams. Finish pockets, if included. Press seams open.

11. For fusible interfacing, apply to wrong side of outer waistband section according to the manufacturer's instructions. Baste sew-in interfacing to wrong side of waistband. If band will not be topstitched, catchstitch interfacing along lengthwise fold line as shown.

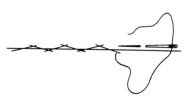

CATCHSTITCH INTERFACING AT WAISTBAND FOLDLINE UNLESS BAND WILL BE TOPSITICHED.

12. With right sides together, pin and stitch interfaced side of waistband to right side of skirt, placing underlay extension at left back. Trim; press.

13. Fold band to the wrong side along upper edge, matching ends. Stitch ends, and stitch lower edges of underlay extension. Trim; turn right side out, and press.

14. Fold under seam allowance on inside of band so fold just covers previous stitching. Press. Trim seam allowance to 1/4" (7 mm). Baste, then stitch from the right side in the "ditch" of the previous stitching line. Topstitch, if desired. Sew hook and eye at ends of band.

Tip: As an alternative for bulky or stiff fabrics, finish the inside of the waistband this way: Mark the seamline on the inner edge of the band and trim seam allowance to 1/4" (.5 cm). Serge the edge or bind with tricot seam binding. Stitch ends to waist seamline. Fold under the corner at each end. Pin, matching seamlines, and stitch from the right side as above.

Hem

15. Open out vent facings and press hem. Open out hems at vent and fold vent facings to right side along foldlines, matching hemlines. Stitch along hemlines. Trim, turn to right side, and press.

16. Clean finish or bind upper edge of hem. Pin, and stitch with hand or machine blind stitch. By hand, stitch facings to hem.

The loose front panel adds a grace note to the long straight linen skirt. With a sleeveless vest and matching overshirt it fills a difficult wardrobe need: an outfit suitable for the office yet still cool and comfortable in summer weather. For casual occasions, wear the top pieces with white linen shorts or pants.

Underneath, the fitted vest from Pattern I adapts readily to blouse status. Instructions are on page 77.

The shirt is made from Pattern A (page 18) with the sleeves shortened to three-quarter length and finished with top-stitched hems. The shoulders are moved slightly forward, a back yoke added, and the lower back made with a center seam to accommodate a vent—details that give the basic pattern a completely different look with little trouble.

To move the shoulders forward, just subtract about 1-1/2" (4 cm) at the shoulder line of the front pattern piece and add it to the yoke. Make the same adjustment to the front and back neck facings. Mark the original location of the shoulder seam on the yoke pattern piece for matching to the sleeve. Instructions for the back yoke are on page 25.

The button-front skirt is made in blue linen (lined to reduce wrinkling), a nice complement to the crisp blouse and jacket of the same fabric.

Lots of topstitching on edges and pockets gives the jacket a well-finished appearance. Out-of-the-ordinary button closures, repeated on the blouse, make a garment that's yours alone. Instructions are in the Embellishments section, page 98.

Make the jacket from Pattern B, adding a back yoke and lowering the front shoulders as described on page 50. The linen jacket will wrinkle less and hang more smoothly if it's lined. Details are on page 114.

This blouse, like the one shown in the preceding photo, is made from Pattern I. It sports small pocket flaps, topstitched in place.

Straight Skirt with Front Panel

The panel is sewed into the right side seam; if you'd like a pocket, put on the left. Free edges of the panel and the skirt hem might be topstitched approximately 1" (2.5 cm) from the edges as shown in the photo, below.

Cut as for skirt above. Add only a left pocket. Cut panel for same finished length as skirt, adding 1-1/4" (3 cm) hem allowance on front and lower edges. Add seam allowance on other sides.

1. Stitch dart at panel upper edge.

2. Hem front and lower edge of panel. Clean finish or bind edges, then press to wrong side along hemlines. Miter the lower corner: Unfold the facing and hem and refold on the diagonal across the intersection of the creases as illustrated, matching the creases. Press this fold, then fold diagonal edges so they meet on the inside. Stitch the folds together by hand.

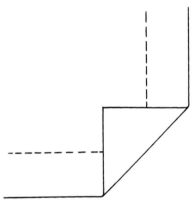

MITER PANEL HEM AT THE LOWER CORNER.

3. Stitch darts in skirt front. With panel wrong side to skirt right side, baste panel to skirt along right side seamline and upper edge.

4. Construct the skirt according to the instructions above, sewing panel into right side and waistline seams.

Button Front Skirt

For continuity of design, add buttons and buttonholes along the back vent too.

CUTTING

Cut according to the layout for skirt without panel, adding seam and hem allowances. Cut waistband as for the plain skirt, but instead of underlay extension at left end add 3/4" (2 cm) at each end for center front overlap, plus seam allowance. Cut waistband interfacing or purchased waistband stay according to the instructions for the plain front skirt.

Cut interfacing for front facings. For fusible, cut without seam allowances. For sew-in, add seam allowances at upper and lower ends and at outer edge.

CONSTRUCTION

1. Stitch darts in skirt fronts and back.

2. To add pockets, see page 91.

3. Fuse interfacing to wrong sides of front facings, with edge of interfacing along front fold line. Press facing hem allowance to wrong side; stitch.

4. For sew-in interfacing, stitch to front facing outer edge with right sides together. Press seam allowances toward facing. Fold interfacing to facing wrong side along seamline; press. Catchstitch invisibly along front foldline if front edges will not be topstitched.

5. Press facings to wrong side along foldlines. Baste across upper edges.

6. With right sides together, stitch center back seam from upper end of vent to upper edge.

7. Finish back vent, stitch side seams, and apply waistband according to the instructions for the plain-front skirt, steps 7 through 14, page 49. Waistband will extend just to front edges.

Hem and finishing

8. Open out facings and press hem in place. Open out hems at facings and fold facings to right side along foldlines, matching hemlines. Stitch along hemlines. Trim, turn to right side, and press.

9. Clean finish or bind upper edge of hem. Pin, and stitch with hand or machine blind stitch. By hand, stitch facings to hem.

10. Topstitch front edges, if desired, along outer edges and close to facing lines.

11. Position and work buttonholes; stitch buttons in place.

Lined Skirt

Lining makes a skirt more comfortable to wear, adds body to lighter fabrics, and improves wrinkle resistance. Choose a lining fabric that's not too heavy for the skirt fabric, and one with the same care requirements.

For lining, cut just the skirt front and back pieces according to the version you are making, adding seam allowances but eliminating the back vent facing extensions. Cut to the skirt hemline, which will allow for a narrow hem in the lining. For the button-front skirt, cut lining front to the front facing line, adding seam allowance to both lining and facing.

1. Construct the skirt according to the instructions to the point of attaching the waistband. For the button front skirt, don't baste front facings across the upper edges until lining is in place.

2. Make the lining: stitch darts in the front and back.

3. Stitch center back seam from slightly above top of vent to slightly below bottom of zipper.

4. Stitch side seams, leaving open above lower ends of pockets.

5. Pin lining to skirt at waist with wrong sides together. Baste.

6. Attach the skirt waistband.

7. Hem the skirt and lining separately.

8. For the button front skirt, press under facing seam allowances, fold facings over lining and stitch by hand, taking care not to catch skirt fabric through the lining.

9. Turn under lining seam allowances along zipper seam and stitch by hand. Finish back vent and along pockets in the same way.

For the panel variation, line the panel too. Cut lining to the panel seamlines at the front and lower edges, and add seam allowance at the side and upper edges. Baste lining to panel wrong side at top and right side. On front and lower edges, tuck lining edges under the panel hems when the hems are sewn.

VARIATIONS

Add buttonholes at upper part of front panel, with buttons on the skirt front. Interface under the portion of the panel hem where the buttonholes will be, and place a small piece of interfacing behind each button for reinforcement.

A B C D E F G H I J

Full Skirt

Cool and breezy in a light summer fabric or comfortably warm in wool, a full skirt is on almost every woman's list of wardrobe necessities. It can be strictly utilitarian in denim, it can be shimmery and luxurious in silk charmeuse, or anything between. The only fitting necessary is at the waistband, so you're ready to sew with minimal preparation.

The skirt is pleated onto the band, with buttons down the front. You can add inseam pockets, and you can make it the length you like best this year.

INSTRUCTIONS

For detailed information about working with the patterns, refer to page 106. The pattern is on page 130.

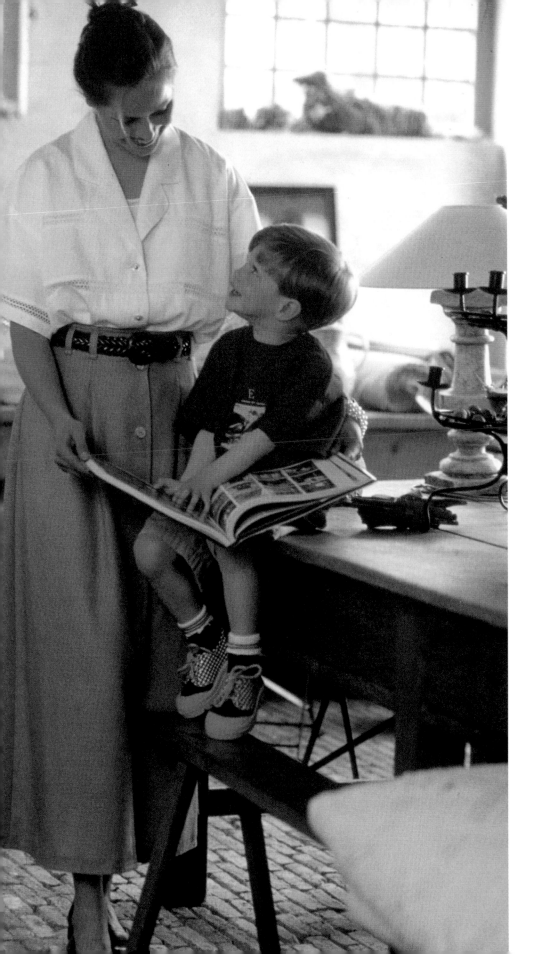

Fresh and crisp for summer, the full skirt in very basic khaki cotton twill goes along with almost any top in the closet. The skirt is the narrowed version, just four pleats across the front, with practical inseam pockets. The waistband is cut wider as a design variation and the belt carriers topstitched across both upper and lower ends to keep the belt centered on the band. The hem is topstitched in place.

Handkerchief linen inset with delicate cotton fagoting adds a distinctively feminine accent to the basic shirt. Details are on pages 94-95.

MATERIALS

Fabric

60" (152 cm):

    All sizes, 2-1/4 yds (2.10 m)

45" (115 cm):

    All sizes, 4-1/4 yds (3.9 m)

Lay out pattern pieces to determine fabric requirements for sizes and fabric widths not given above, if substantial alterations are made, or if fabric has a pattern that must be matched.

Other Materials

- Waistband interfacing, 1-1/4" (3.2 cm) wide
- Interfacing for skirt front, 1-1/4 yds (1.15 m)
- Buttons for the front
- Lining material for inner pockets (optional), 3/8 yd (.35 m)

CUTTING

Add seam and hem allowances to all pattern pieces before cutting.

For 60" (152 cm) fabric, cut on fabric folded lengthwise as shown in the layout. With 45" (115 cm) fabric, the back cannot be cut as a single piece. Cut two from single thickness fabric as shown, adding seam allowance at center back. As an alternative, narrow the pattern according to the instructions following the construction steps.

Cut waistband to a length of 28", 29", 30", 31-3/4" (71, 73.5, 76.5, 80.5 cm), and 2-1/2" (6.5 cm) wide, plus seam allowances on all sides. Cut fusible waistband interfacing 1-1/4" (3.2 cm) wide and to finished band length. Cut sew-in interfacing 1-1/4" (3.2 cm) wide plus one seam allowance, and finished length of band with seam allowance added for both ends. Transfer pattern markings to garment pieces.

Cut two front interfacing strips the width of the pattern front facing. For fusible, add only a narrow hem allowance at the outer edge. For sew-in, add seam allowances at upper and inner edges only; do not add hem allowance.

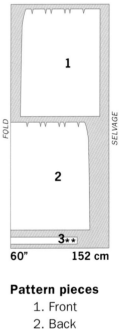

60"   152 cm

Pattern pieces

  1. Front

  2. Back

**3. Waistband

**Pattern piece not provided. Finished measurements are given with the cutting instructions; the first measurement is for the smallest size, followed by measurements for subsequently larger sizes.

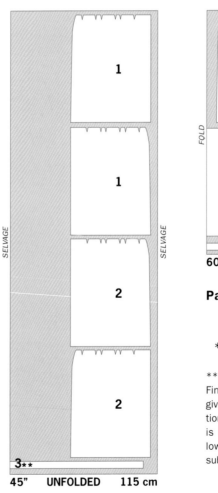

45"   UNFOLDED   115 cm

CONSTRUCTION

For some of the steps below, additional information can be found in the Sewing Techniques section that begins on page 111. Instructions for pockets begin on page 89. To add waistband belt carriers, see page 112.

Facings

1. Fuse interfacing to wrong sides of front facings, with edge of interfacing along front fold line. Press facing hem allowance to wrong side; stitch.

2. For sew-in interfacing, stitch to front facing outer edge with right sides together. Press seam allowances toward facing. Fold interfacing to facing wrong side along seamline; press. Catchstitch invisibly along front foldline or topstitch front edges later.

3. Press facings to wrong side along foldlines. Baste across upper edges.

Back and side seams and pleats

4. For back cut as two pieces, stitch center back seam.

5. Sew fronts to back at side seamlines, right sides together. To add pockets, see page 141.

6. Form pleats around skirt upper edge. Baste.

Waistband

7. Baste or fuse interfacing to wrong side of band between waist seamline and lengthwise center. For fusible, follow manufacturer's instructions. For sew-in, trim close to basting on ends and long edge.

8. Fold band wrong side out, ends and edges aligned, and stitch ends from fold to waist seamline. Trim and press, turn right side out.

9. Pin right side (interfaced side) of band to right side of skirt, band ends at front edges, adjusting pleats if necessary. Stitch. Trim and grade seam allowances; press toward band.

10. Fold under seam allowance on inside of band so fold just covers previous stitching. Press. Trim seam allowance to 1/4" (7 mm). Baste, then stitch from the right side in the "ditch" of the previous stitching line.

Tip: As an alternative for bulky or stiff fabrics, finish the inside of the waistband this way: Mark the seamline on the inner edge of the band and trim seam allowance to 1/4" (.5 cm). Serge the edge or bind with tricot seam binding. Fold under the corner at each end. Pin, matching seamlines, and stitch from the right side as above.

11. Topstitch outer edges of band.

Hem and finishing

12. Open out facings at lower edge. Press hem. Clean finish raw edge.

13. Fold facing to wrong side along facing foldline, aligning hemlines. Stitch facing to skirt along hem crease. Trim, turn to right side, and press.

14. Pin and stitch hem with hand or machine blindstitch. As an alternative, make the hem fairly narrow and topstitch it along with the front edges.

15. Topstitch front edges of skirt.

16. Mark and stitch buttonholes on skirt right side along center front line and on waistband. Sew on buttons.

Reducing the fullness

The skirt front and back can be cut narrower to fit 45" (115 cm) fabric without a center back seam, or if you would simply like less fullness in the skirt.

Fold a lengthwise pleat about at the center of the back pattern piece, parallel to the lengthwise grainline, so the piece fits the doubled fabric. Pleat the front piece the same way.

Keep in mind that the skirt will be reduced in width a total of eight times the width of the pleat.

Respace the pleats at the top, and blend the waistline edge to match the waistline of the original pattern.

Together, the indigo linen skirt and shirt create the effect of a classic shirt-waist dress. Each teams up just as well with other wardrobe pieces: the shirt equally classic with natural linen pants or a long straight skirt, and the skirt with a basic white tee and perhaps a brilliantly colored linen vest, or one in an outrageous print.

The shirt (Pattern A) is given a distinctive look with the addition of a front yoke, box pleated patch pockets, and lots of topstitching. The pocket flaps are sewn into the yoke seam; the upper edge of the pocket 3/4" (2 cm) below.

To add a front yoke, cut the pattern straight across, perpendicular to center front and about 2" (5 cm) above the bust. Add seam allowances at both cut edges.

Cut a separate front facing at the facing foldline, adding seam allowances here to both pieces too. Reassemble the front, incorporating the pocket flap, and stitch the facing to the front along the former foldline. Then construct the shirt just like the basic model, page 18.

Knit shorts and tee go from deck to town topped with a full skirt in soft white cotton pique. French seams and a machine-stitched hem provide a neat finish in case beach breezes reveal the skirt's wrong side.

The shorts are cut from Pattern F. The shirt was made to button down the front, with a front facing added. Here's how:

Make a new copy of the shirt front pattern. Draw a line parallel to the center front, 5/8" (1.5 cm) outside it, for the facing seamline.

Draw the facing line on the pattern, adding a front facing the same width as the neck facing. Blend the front facing line into the neck facing line at the front/neck corner.

Follow the instructions for the Pattern B shirt to construct this one. Read, too, Sewing with Knits, page 37.

Tailored Trousers

To find a pattern for classic pants that fit well and look great in all kinds of fabrics is a sewer's dream. This pair is traditional in style and fit, with double front pleats, back darts, and a front fly zipper. Front pockets are cut in at the front hip. To make inseam pockets, as shown in the drawing, refer to the pocket instructions on page 91. The legs are moderately wide—the medium size is 21-1/2" (54.5) cm) around the hemline—and can be narrowed or widened. And it's easy to add cuffs if you'd like them.

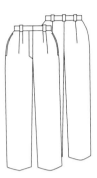

INSTRUCTIONS

Detailed information about using the patterns in on page 106. The pattern is on page 134.

MATERIALS

Fabric

LONG PANTS WITHOUT CUFFS

45" (115 cm):

Size XXS, 2-7/8 yds (2.65 m)

Size XL, 3 yds (2.75 m)

60" (152 cm):

Size XXS 1-5/8 yds (1.50 m)

Size XL, 2-5/8 yds (2.40 m)

SHORTS

45" (115 cm):

Size XXS, 1-3/4 yds (1.60 m)

Size XL, 1-7/8 yds (1.75 m)

60" (152 cm):

Size XXS, 1-3/8 yds (1.30 m)

Size XL, 1-1/2 yds (1.40 m)

Lay out pattern pieces to determine fabric requirements for sizes and fabric widths not given above, if substantial alterations are made, or if fabric has a pattern that must be matched.

Other Materials

- Lining fabric, 1/4 yd (.25 m), for pocket facings
- Stabilizing tape for pocket edges
- Waistband interfacing
- Zipper, 7" to 9" (18 cm to 22 cm)
- Hooks and eyes for the waistband

Patterned fabrics, all in navy and cream, add fun to wardrobe planning. Each of these cottons combines with its own favorite solid-colored partner for easy summer dressing. The pants have inseam pockets and a front zipper. The vest can be made with Pattern I, a belt sewn in at the side seams. For the shirt, Pattern A goes to a new length.

CUTTING

Add seam and hem allowances to all pieces before cutting.

Cut two of piece 1 and two of piece 2 from doubled fabric as shown on the layout. Cut waistband from single fabric thickness on crosswise grain, or from lengthwise grain for stretchy fabrics. Finished waistband measurements: 2-1/2' (6.5 cm) wide and in length 26", 26-3/4", 27-1/2", 28-3/4", 30-1/2", 32", 33-1/2" (66, 68, 70, 73, 77, 81, 85 cm). Add seam allowance at all edges. Cut two pocket back pieces from garment fabric and two pocket facings from lining. For belt carriers, cut a lengthwise strip 14" 36 cm) long and 1-1/4" (3 cm) wide (includes seam allowances). Transfer all pattern markings to garment pieces.

Cut two pieces of stabilizer tape the length of the pocket edge seamline. Cut waistband interfacing 1-1/4" (3 cm) wide to band length.

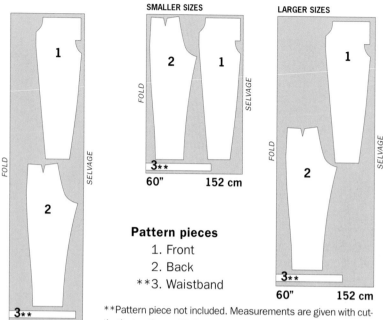

Pattern pieces

1. Front
2. Back
**3. Waistband

**Pattern piece not included. Measurements are given with cutting instructions, with the measurement for the smallest size given first, followed by measurements for subsequently larger sizes.

Pocket pieces are in the pocket pattern section, page 141.

CONSTRUCTION

For some of the steps below, additional information can be found in the Sewing Techniques section that begins on page 111.

Pleats and darts

1. Stitch and press darts in back pieces.

2. Fold front pleats with outer pleat toward side. Baste across at waist seamline.

Zipper

3. Mark zipper placement on center front seamlines. Allow 1/4" (.5 cm) between zipper top and waistline seam, and mark bottom of zipper below stop. Stitch fronts together along crotch seam for several inches (6-8 cm) below lower end of zipper.

4. Fold left front fly extension to inside, folding 3/8" (1 cm) outside center front. Press. Fold right fly extension to inside along center front line; press and baste.

5. Open the zipper and place face up against wrong side of pants left front, with the fabric fold a scant 1/8" (2 mm) from the zipper teeth. Baste. Stitch close to the fold. Close the zipper.

6. Baste right front over left front, matching centers.

7. Fold back pants right front; baste and stitch right side of zipper to fly extension only, stitching along the raised thread in the zipper tape.

8. On the outside, mark the lower end of the zipper. Topstitch the pants right side through all layers approximately 1" (2.5 cm) from center front, curving the stitching to end just below the zipper. Reinforce this point with a few wide zigzag stitches, stitch length set at 0.

Pockets

9. Stitch pocket facings to pants front sections with right sides together, incorporating a strip of stabilizer tape in the seam to prevent stretching. Press flat, seam allowances toward facing. Press to inside along seamline. Topstitch on the outside, or understitch facing to seam allowances 3/16" (.5 cm) from seamline.

Tailored pants are equally classic whether short or long. Winter shorts, in corduroy, wool flannel, or synthetic suede, are very proper—and perfectly comfortable—worn with opaque tights. It's easy to add cuffs to shorts or long pants; instructions are on page 114. Wool melton, orange as October, is ideal for the Pattern H jacket.

Light and airy cotton gauze is just the fabric for the widened version of the tailored pants. Elastic at the waist makes them quick to put together. Tunic Pattern B makes an ideal beach shirt. Button it up and belt it with a bright sash, and it's a perfect dress for lunch on the pier.

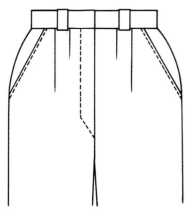

POCKETS CUT IN AT THE HIP FRONT ARE TRADITIONAL ON TAILORED PANTS.

10. Pin the under pockets behind the pocket facings, right side of under pocket toward facing. Stitch around curved outer edges. Overcast the seams. Baste pocket to seam allowance at upper front edge and side.

Leg and crotch seams

11. Pin front to back at outer leg seams; stitch.

12. Pin front to back at inner leg seams; stitch.

13. Turn one leg wrong side out and pull it into the other leg, right side out, matching inner and outer seamlines. Pin remaining section of crotch seam; stitch.

Belt carriers

14. Fold fabric strip in half lengthwise, right side out; press. Fold raw edges in to first fold; press. Stitch close to both edges.

15. Cut the strip into segments 1-3/4" (4.5 cm) long.

16. Pin carriers to waist, end aligned with pants upper edge. Place one between each pair of front pleats, one at each back dart, and one at center back. Baste.

Waistband

17. Baste interfacing to wrong side of band between waist seamline and lengthwise center. Trim seam allowances from ends.

18. Fold band wrong side out, ends and edges aligned, and stitch ends from fold to waist seamline. Trim and press, turn right side out.

19. Pin and stitch right side (interfaced side) of band to right side of skirt. Trim and grade seam allowances; press toward band.

20. Fold under seam allowance on inside of band so fold just covers previous stitching. Press. Trim seam allowance to 1/4" (7 mm). Baste, then stitch from the right side in the "ditch" of the previous stitching line.

TIP: As an alternative for bulky or stiff fabrics, finish the inside of the waistband this way: Mark the seamline on the inner edge of the band and trim seam allowance to 1/4" (.5 cm). Serge the edge or bind with tricot seam binding. Fold under the corner at each end. Pin, matching seamlines, and stitch from the right side as above.

21. Turn under 1/2" (1 cm) on carrier raw ends and pin to band so that folds are even with upper edge of band. Check that belt will slide easily through carriers, but that they are not too loose. Adjust and trim unfinished ends slightly, if necessary.

22. Slipping machine presser foot under loop of carrier, zigzag stitch end securely in place.

23. Fold and press hems in legs. Clean finish or bind upper edges. Pin hems, and stitch with hand or machine blind stitch.

Pants with Tapered Legs

1. Determine the desired finished width of the pants leg at the hemline (be sure it's wide enough to slip over your heel). Subtract this figure from finished hemline width of Pattern G leg in your size. Divide the difference by 4.

2. On the hemlines of the original front and back pattern pieces, measure in from each side by the amount figured in step 1. Mark these points.

3. Draw a line from a point about 2" (5 cm) below the crotch point from the side seamline to the outer marked hemline point. Draw a line from the same point on the inseam to the other hemline point. When adding hem allowance, remember the leg seamlines must taper to the same degree in the opposite direction. Fold the pattern along the hemline and match the hem portion of the side seams to those of the leg.

4. Add facing for the side slit. For a slit 1-1/2" (3 cm) long and hem and facing 1" (2.5 cm) wide, for example, cut an outward extension 1-1/2" (4 cm) wide on the outer seam of the front and back legs, beginning 1-1/2" (4 cm) above the hemline and continuing to the lower edge. Add 1-1/2" (4 cm) hem allowance. Taper the upper end of the extension to the normal seam allowance as shown.

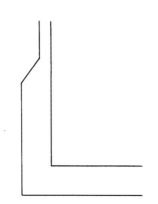

EXTEND SIDE SEAM ALLOWANCES TO
MAKE VENT FACING.

5. Make the pants according to the instructions, leaving the outer leg seams open below a point 1/2" (1.5 cm) below the tops of the facings.

6. Fold under 1/2" (1.5 cm) on the facings and hems. Press; stitch close to fold.

7. Press facings to inside along the seamlines. Press hem.

8. Miter the corners. Unfold the facing and hem at a corner and refold on the diagonal across the intersection of the creases as illustrated, matching the creases. Press this fold, then fold diagonal edges so they meet on the inside. Stitch the folds together by hand.

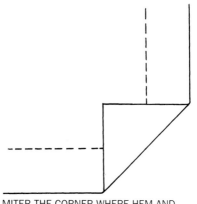

MITER THE CORNER WHERE HEM AND
VENT FACING MEET.

9. Stitch the hems by hand or machine. Reinforce across the upper end of each slit with a bar tack or a few machine zigzag stitches.

Wide Legs and Elasticized Waist

This variation works only with soft, light fabrics with good draping qualities, such as lightweight rayon, sandwashed silk, and very soft cotton. Inseam pockets (page 91) are the best choice with this style. In addition to the fabric, you will need waistband elastic cut to your waist measurement, or flat-sewn elastic as long as upper edge of pants, plus seam allowances.

1. Pin the front pocket underlay to the pants front before making hip width adjustments.

2. This style should be somewhat loose through the hips. Add approximately 1/4" (.5 cm) at the side front and side back seamlines from the waistline to just above the crotch line for a total of 1" (2 cm) additional hip ease.

3. To widen the leg slightly (overdoing it will give you bell bottoms), extend the hemline of the basic pattern outward by about 1" (2.5 cm) and mark this point. Draw a line to connect the lower end of the new upper side seam to the marked point. Widen by about half this amount on the inseam, tapering from an inch or so below the crotch seamline. Be sure to add the same amount to both front and back pattern pieces.

4. Extend the pattern pieces upward at the waistline. For elastic to go into a casing, add twice the width of the elastic plus 3/8" (1 cm) ease plus hem allowance. For elastic that is sewn flat, add the width of the elastic plus hem allowance.

5. Add seam and hem allowances, then cut front and back from doubled fabric.

6. Stitch a pocket lining section to each front and back. Press seam allowances toward pocket. Understitch lining to seam allowances, stitching approximately 3/16" (.5 cm) from seamline.

7. Stitch front to back at side seams above and below pocket opening. Stitch pocket lining sections together, starting and ending at side seamlines. Press pockets toward front. Baste to pants front across upper edges. If desired, topstitch front pocket edges.

8. Stitch front to back at inseams.

9. Turn one leg right side out and insert it into the other leg, which is wrong side out. Pin and stitch the crotch seam. If Flat-sewn elastic will be used, stitch the lower end of the back crotch seam. Turn under and press the hem allowance on the waist facing. Position the elastic band and stitch it in place. Draw up and tie the elastic threads, then complete the back crotch seam, incorporating the elastic ends into the stitching line.

10. For elastic in a casing, Fold under the waist facing hem after completing the crotch seam. Fold upper edge to the waistline and stitch close to the edge, leaving an opening of 2" (5 cm) or so at center back. Thread elastic through the casing. Stitch ends together securely. Stitch across the opening.

11. Press and stitch hems.

A B C D E F G H I J

The Essential Jacket

Most every wardrobe depends upon a good jacket or two. Make an everyday, go-with-everything version, and another to wear when you want to be noticed.

This pattern is basic enough that you can quickly make it up in a dozen different ways. The lined jacket is long and loose-fitting. Front darts and pleats under the back belt shape the waistline. It can be made with or without a collar, and with or without vents to accent the two-piece sleeves. Instructions call for patch pockets, but pocket style can be varied as you wish.

INSTRUCTIONS

Detailed information about using the patterns is on page 106.
The pattern is on page 136.

Rich-colored wool plaid makes a jacket that's destined for frequent wear. The pattern is beautifully matched across the front to the sleeves, at the pockets, and on the lower sleeves. (For more about matching plaids, see page 115) The pants, from Pattern G, are lightweight synthetic suede.

MATERIALS

Fabric
JACKET WITHOUT COLLAR

60" (152 cm):

All sizes, 1-7/8 yds (1.75 m)

JACKET WITH COLLAR

60" (152 cm):

All sizes, 2-1/8 yds (1.95 m)

Lay out pattern pieces to determine fabric requirements for sizes and fabric widths not given above, if substantial alterations are made, or if fabric has a pattern that must be matched.

Lining
EITHER VERSION

45" (115 cm):

Size XXS/XS, 2-1/4 yds (2.10 m)

Size L/XL, 2-1/2 yds (2.30 m)

Other Materials
- Interfacing, fusible or sew-in, 1-1/4 yds (1.15 m)
- Stabilizer tape
- Shoulder pads with attached sleeve heads
- Buttons for front, sleeves, and back belt

CUTTING

Add seam and hem allowances to all pieces before cutting, except where indicated. Transfer all pattern markings to garment pieces.

Fold fabric lengthwise and cut pieces as shown on the layout. For piece 8, the back belt, cut one from lining material if outer fabric is bulky. At lower edge of piece 1 add 1-1/4" (3 cm) hem allowance from side to facing seamline. From facing seamline on around, add seam allowance. Add the same hem allowance at lower edges of pieces 2, 4, and 5. Cut piece 3 using pattern piece 1, and piece 7 with pattern piece 2, adding seam allowances.

Cut lining with pieces 1, 2, 4, and 5. Add seam allowances, but do not add hem allowances at lower edges. Cut pieces 1 and 2 with the facing seamlines as the outer lining seamlines. Eliminate the sleeve vent extensions on pieces 4 and 5. Fold fabric lengthwise as for jacket. Place piece 2 with center back line 3/4" (2 cm) from fabric fold. Do not cut along the center back line; continue the neckline edge and the lower edge to the fabric fold.

Cut fusible interfacing: two from piece 3, one from piece 6 and piece 8. Do not add seam allowances.

Cut tape stays for neck back and shoulder seams, cutting to the pattern pieces.

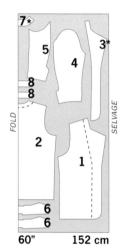

Pattern pieces:

1. Front
2. Back
*3. Front facing
4. Upper sleeve
5. Under sleeve
6. Collar
*7. Back neck facing
8. Belt

*These pieces are cut from other pattern pieces as described in the cutting instructions.

Jacket with Collar

Take time to press each seam and stitching line neatly, especially if the jacket is made of wool.

For some of the construction steps below, additional information can be found in the Sewing Techniques sections that begins on page 111.

Interfacing, fronts and back

1. Fuse interfacing to wrong sides of front facings, outer belt section, and one collar section (this will be the under collar), following manufacturer's instructions.

2. Stitch darts in front pieces; stitch pleats in back.

3. Make lined patch pockets following the instructions on page 92. Stitch them in place on jacket fronts.

4. Stitch back belt sections with right sides together, leaving an opening on one long edge for turning. Trim; turn right side out. Press, and top-stitch edges.

5. Position belt on jacket back over the pleat stitching. Sew a button at each end through all layers.

6. Stitch back to front at shoulder seams, incorporating a tape stay in the seamline to prevent stretching.

Facings and collar

7. Stitch tape stay to back neckline, stitching in the seam allowance just outside the seamline.

8. Stitch under collar to neck edge, right sides together, beginning and ending stitching exactly at collar end seamlines. Match markings and clip neck edge to tape stitching line as necessary.

9. With right sides together, stitch front facings to back neck facing at shoulders. Stay stitch the facing neck edge, using a moderate stitch length and stitching along the seamline.

10. Pin upper collar to facing neck edge, right sides together, matching markings and centers. Stitch between collar end seamlines, clipping facing neck edge as necessary.

11. Right sides together, pin facing and upper collar to jacket and under collar. Stitch. Trim and press.

12. Turn facing to inside; turn collar right side out. Press.

13. Match collar/neck seamlines under back facing. Stitch seam allowances loosely together by hand.

Side seams and sleeves

14. Stitch back to front at side seams, matching markings and easing front fullness.

15. With right sides together, stitch upper sleeve to under sleeve, matching markings and easing fullness. Leave seam open below upper end of vent.

16. Hem lower edges of sleeves, trimming hem allowance under upper sleeve vent facing. Fold upper sleeve vent facing to inside along sleeve seamline. Position over under sleeve vent facing, matching seamlines, and sew buttons through all thicknesses.

17. Ease stitch sleeve caps between matching points. Lengthen stitch slightly and stitch just inside, then just outside the seamline. Draw up bobbin threads to fit sleeve to jacket.

18. Pin sleeve to jacket, right sides together, matching markings and shoulders. Note that sleeve seams and jacket seam do not match. Stitch. Trim underarm seam allowance; press upper seam allowance lightly toward sleeve.

19. Try on the jacket and pin shoulder pads in place, outer edges extending to the edges of seam allowances at shoulders. Tack loosely in place.

Lining

20. Make back pleat. On wrong side, fold piece along center back. Stitch on wrong side, 3/4" (2 cm) from fold, down 1-1/2" (4 cm) from top and up 2" (5 cm) from lower edge. Press to one side.

A collarless jacket is just right with a big scarf or high collar. Subtle gray wool tweed works perfectly for a jacket that can go anywhere.

The front neckline is raised slightly for an elongated effect. It's an easy design change: Just move the neckline curve upward by approximately 2" (5 cm), maintaining the center front line and outer seamline. Blend the new neckline smoothly to the original an inch or so below the shoulder.

Dispel the gloom of a dreary day with bright sherbet colors! This jacket goes together quickly; it's stitched to the facing and lining at the outer edges, then trimmed with wool braid.

The skirt is a short rendition of Pattern D in wool double knit. The hem is pressed to the inside, then topstitched in place on the outside with a double needle.

21. With right sides together, stitch fronts to back at shoulders and sides. Stitch sleeve seams.

22. Ease stitch upper sleeve edges. Pin and stitch sleeves to lining.

23. Stay stitch the lining front and neck edges.

24. Pin lining to jacket facings with right sides together. Stitch, beginning and ending approximately 6" (15 cm) above the jacket lower edge.

25. At the lower edge, match lining edge to edge of jacket hem. Pin, and stitch by hand. A pleat will form across the lower lining. At lining edges, turn under lining seam allowances and finish stitching lining to facing.

26. Attach sleeve linings in the same way.

Finishing

27. Try on the jacket and fold collar and lapels smoothly into place. Topstitch front edges and lower edges to facing line. Topstitch collar. Mark button and buttonhole placement. Uppermost button should be just below lower end of lapel roll; lower one approximately 3" (15 cm) above the lower edge. Jacket buttonholes are usually horizontal, their outer ends 1/8" (.5 cm) outside the center front line. Buttons are sewed along the center line.

28. Topstitch jacket outer edges. Stitch on the outside from the lower point of the lapel roll, around the front corner, to the edge of the facing. Stitch on the facing side up the lapels and around the upper collar.

29. Work buttonholes and sew on buttons.

Jacket without Collar

Cut pieces as for the jacket above, using the alternate seamlines on the pattern pieces and omitting the collars. Construct it as above, too, but stitch facings to the jacket neckline without collar.

Jacket with Bound Edges

Without collar or facings, and with a simple finish to the edges, this is a quick jacket to make. In addition to wool fabric and lining you will need wool foldover braid, sold in fabric stores that stock Austrian boiled wool. As a substitute, bind the edges with bias strips of a non-raveling wool fabric. Measure outer edge, sleeve hemlines, and pocket widths to determine yardage needed. You will also need basting liquid or a roll of narrow fusible web.

CUTTING

Follow cutting lines on the pattern for the collarless jacket, above. For front and back, do not add hem allowances or seam allowances at outer edges. Cut sleeve to hemline, omitting vent facings. Do not cut front or back neck facings.

Cut front lining the same as the outer jacket front, and sleeve lining the same as the jacket sleeve. To cut back lining, place the pattern piece with center back line 3'4" (2 cm) from fabric fold. Do not cut along the center back line; continue the neckline edge and the lower edge to the fabric fold. Don't add seam allowance at the neck edge, or hem allowance.

Pockets for this jacket are slightly different from the standard patch pocket. Cut both lining and pocket to the pocket upper hemline, adding seam allowance on the other sides. Trim a scant 1/8" (2 mm) from sides and lower edge of lining.

Cut fusible interfacing according to the front and back neck facing patterns, without seam or hem allowances.

Cut braid exactly by pattern outer edge seamlines and lower edge hemlines. For the jacket outer edge trim, piece braid as necessary to make a single strip. Mark on the braid all jacket seamlines, centers, and other reference points. Allow 1/2" (1 cm) at each end for overlap. Cut strips for sleeve hemlines and upper pocket edges, allowing extra at ends.

As an alternative, cut bias strips 1-1/4" (3 cm) wide from wool or another fabric that ravels very little. Stitch ends with right sides together as shown on page 73 to make up the total length needed. Fold the strip lengthwise, not quite in half, right side out, and press. Attach it to the jacket like braid, above, with the shorter edge of the trim on the jacket's right side. Stitch.

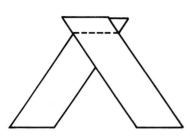

SEW WITH THE FABRIC GRAIN TO PIECE BIAS STRIPS, OFFSETTING THEM BY THE WIDTH OF THE SEAM ALLOWANCE.

CONSTRUCTION

1. Fuse interfacing to wrong sides of fronts, at back neck, and to facings and outer belt section.

2. Stitch darts in jacket front. Stitch pleats in back. On wrong side, press pleats toward sides.

3. Sew pocket to lining, right sides together, on sides and lower edge, easing pocket to fit to lining. Trim; press seam allowances toward lining. Turn right side out and baste layers together close to upper edge.

4. Press under the ends of a pocket trim strip. Working from the wrong side, fold the braid tightly over the pocket edge with the wider side of the braid on the inside of the pocket. Use a few drops of basting liquid to hold the braid in place, or press in small pieces of fusible web at intervals. On the right side, stitch close to the edge of the trim.

5. Position the pockets on the jacket fronts, baste, and topstitch in place.

6. Follow instructions for the jacket with collar, steps 4 through 7, to make the belt and stitch the shoulder seams.

Side seams and sleeves

7. Stitch back to front at side seams, matching markings and easing front fullness.

8. With right sides together, stitch upper sleeve to under sleeve, matching markings and easing fullness.

9. Ease stitch sleeve caps between matching points. Lengthen stitch slightly and stitch just inside, then just outside the seamline. Draw up bobbin threads to fit sleeve to jacket.

10. Pin sleeve to jacket, right sides together, matching markings and shoulders. Note that sleeve seams and jacket seams do not match. Stitch. Trim underarm seam allowance; press upper seam allowance lightly toward sleeve.

11. Try on the jacket and pin shoulder pads in place, outer edges extending to the edges of seam allowances at shoulders. Tack loosely in place.

Lining

12. Make the lining as described in steps 20 through 22 for the jacket with collar.

13. Place lining into jacket with wrong sides together. Pin, and machine baste lining to jacket around all outer edges, stitching close to edges.

Finishing

14. Beginning at a side seamline, apply braid to jacket outer edges and sleeves. Overlap ends and zigzag across the raw edge.

15. Mark and work buttonholes as for the jacket with collar.

Fitted Vest

With half a dozen snazzy vests to enliven the basic skirt, pants, and shirt, you can create the illusion of a far more extensive wardrobe. From the sewer's viewpoint, a vest is the ideal garment: It can be assembled in an evening, it requires little expenditure for fabric, and it offers unlimited potential for creative expression.

Add ties in back, or a belt with buttons or a buckle. Make belt or tie sections first, finishing one end of each section. Sew the unfinished ends into the back dart seams.

INSTRUCTIONS

The instructions are for a lined vest. Lining enhances the outer fabric and makes the garment hang more smoothly. And it's easier to make a vest with a lining – facings and hems, then, are unnecessary. The pattern is on page 138.

MATERIALS

Fabric
45" (115 cm):
  Size XS, 1-1/8 yds (1.05 m)
  Size XL, 1-1/4 yds (1.15 m)
60" (152 cm):
  All sizes, 3/4 yds (.70 m)
Lay out pattern pieces to determine fabric requirements for sizes and fabric widths not given above, if substantial alterations are made, or if fabric has a pattern that must be matched.

Other Materials
- Lining, yardage requirement is the same as for outer fabric
- Buttons for the front
- Interfacing, for very soft or stretchy fabrics, approximately 1 yd (.95 m)

With a very special piece of fabric and about two hours' time, you'll have a vest that makes an eye-catching ensemble of the simplest skirt and blouse. When the fabric is fairly heavy, like this tapestry, use the lighter lining for the back, too. Look for unusual vest fabrics in off-beat places. Flea markets, antique shops, upholstery outlets, and consignment shops can produce some wonderful surprises.

CUTTING

Add seam allowances to all pieces before cutting.

Fold fabric in half lengthwise and cut pieces as shown. Cut lining pieces the same. Cut interfacing to facing lines as shown (Omit armhole interfacing except with very unstable fabrics). For sew-in, add seam allowance at front, neckline, and lower edges.

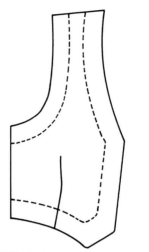

USE THE DOTTED LINES AS A GUIDE FOR CUTTING VEST FACINGS AND INTERFACING.

Transfer all pattern markings to garment pieces. Lightly mark the side seamlines on the right sides of the lining pieces.

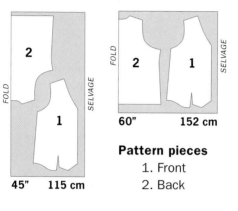

Pattern pieces
1. Front
2. Back

CONSTRUCTION

For some of the construction steps below, additional information can be found in the Sewing Techniques section that begins on page 111.

1. For front interfacing: cut along dart seamlines, abut edges, stitch together with a bridging stitch, or zigzag stitch a piece of seam or hem tape over the join.

2. Stitch darts in fronts and back.

3. Baste or fuse interfacing to wrong sides of fronts. For fusible, follow manufacturer's instructions.

4. Stitch fronts to back at shoulders with right sides together.

5. Staystitch back neck in the seam allowance close to seamline.

6. Stitch lining the same way.

7. With right sides together, stitch vest to lining around fronts and neck, and around armholes. Trim and grade seam allowances. Press seam allowances toward lining as best you can.

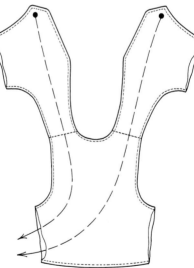

TURN THE VEST RIGHT SIDE OUT THROUGH AN OPEN SIDE BACK SEAM.

8. Turn right side out by pulling both lower front corners through the same side seam opening as shown.

9. Pin outer vest front and back together at side seam, starting at the center of the side and matching the armhole. Stitch, continuing stitching for 1" to 2" (3 cm to 5 cm) along the lining side seam. Stitch the lower half of the seam, matching seamlines at the lower edge, and continuing along the lining seam as at the top. Press seam open.

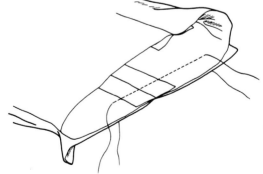

STITCH OUTER VEST SIDE SEAMS FROM CENTER ACROSS UNDERARM LINING SEAM, AND FROM CENTER ACROSS LOWER LINING SEAM.

10. Match lining seamlines and stitch seam closed by hand.

11. Topstitch around outer edges to keep lining in place.

To add facings, follow guidelines below for the blouse facing, but don't raise the armhole. With most fabrics it wouldn't be necessary to add an armhole facing. If facings are added, cut interfacing from the facing pattern too.

Reversible Vest

To make a vest with twice the impact, choose a complementary fabric instead of traditional lining for the reverse side. Take care to stitch the "lining" side seams very neatly. Sew a button on each side at each position, stitching them loosely together through the fabric layers.

Tip: If the inner and outer fabrics are different colors, use one thread color for the needle and the other for the bobbin when topstitching and making buttonholes.

Sleeveless Waistcoat Blouse

Lay out pattern pieces to determine yardage requirements.

PATTERN ADJUSTMENTS AND CUTTING

1. Raise armholes slightly, if necessary for modesty's sake. Taper from underarm seam to matching points.

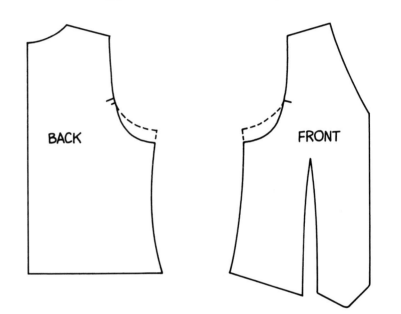

TO MAKE A BLOUSE FROM THE VEST, RAISE THE UNDERARMS AND ADD FACINGS

2. Make a pattern for armhole facing. Use front and back pattern pieces to trace the seamlines. make the facing approximately 1-1/4" (3 cm) wide.

3. Make a back neck facing the same way.

4. Make a front facing. Use the illustration above as a guide. Finished width along the front should be approximately 2" to 2-1/2" (5 to 6 cm). Taper it to the width of the back neck facing where they meet at the shoulder. Draw a curve to join center front and lower front lines. Fold along dart seamlines and tape darts in place.

5. Make a facing pattern for the lower back. Match width to front facing width at side seams. Fold and tape darts as for the front.

CONSTRUCTION

1. Sew or fuse interfacing to facing pieces. Clean finish outer edges.

2. Stitch darts in vest fronts and back.

3. Sew fronts to back at shoulders.

4. Stitch front facings to back neck facings at shoulder ends, right sides together. Stitch front facings to lower back facing at side seamlines.

Blanket fabric – appropriately edged with hand-worked blanket stitch – makes a practical extra layer for cold weather. Darts would interfere with the stripe pattern, so they were eliminated from this vest. Just fold the pattern to bring the dart lines together, and tape them in place to cut the fabric. Straighten the side seams at the waist. Lengthen the vest slightly, and cut it straight across the lower edge.

A few simple pattern changes can create an entirely different garment. The coolest possible pajamas for summer, sewn in delicate cotton lawn, are made with the vest pattern's blouse variation. For the shorts, use Pattern F.

5. Stitch armhole facings together at shoulder seamlines.

6. With right sides together, stitch armhole facings to garment, matching shoulders. Clip and trim seam allowances; press toward facings. Understitch to within 2-1/2" (6 cm) of underarms, stitching facing to seam allowance 3/16" (.5 cm) from seamline.

7. Stitch fronts to back at side seams, continuing seam to edges of armhole facings. Understitch remainder of facing.

8. Pin outer edge facing to blouse, with right sides together, matching shoulders and side seamlines. Stitch. Trim and grade seam allowances.

9. Understitch facings to seam allowances, or press facings to inside and topstitch around outer edges.

Add Sleeves to Make a Blouse

With the front extended into sleeves, the vest becomes a casual summer blouse or a comfortable top for lounging or sleeping. We have omitted the darts for this variation, lengthened the vest, and cut it straight across the lower edge. Make the change this way:

1. On the front pattern piece, draw a straight line from center front to the side/underarm point, keeping it exactly perpendicular to the center front line. Extend this line to a point 1-1/2" (4 cm) past the underarm point. Mark this point A.

2. From A, draw a line straight down, parallel with center front. Make this line 18" (46 cm) long, or desired length. On this line, mark a point 2" (5 cm) below point A and label it B.

3. From the lower end of the new side seamline, draw a perpendicular line to the front seamline. Extend center and front seamline to this line.

4. Extend the shoulder seamline outward to a point 10-1/2" (27 cm) beyond the original shoulder/armhole point. Mark point C at the outer end of this line.

5. From C, draw a perpendicular line 9" (23 cm) long. Mark point D at the lower end of this line.

6. Draw a line from D to B. Round off the inner corner as shown.

7. For the back, make a tracing of the original pattern (leave extra paper around the edges) and place it over the new front piece, matching centers lines and underarms. Mark the back shoulder line (it is slightly higher than the front), extending it to match the front at sleeve hemline. Trace the front hemline, underarm, side seamline, and lower edge onto the new back pattern piece.

8. Make a front/neck facing and a back neck facing following the guidelines for the vest facings. The front facing should end at the shirt lower edge.

Remember to add seam and hem allowances to all pieces before cutting. For facings, use a very lightweight fusible interfacing and overcast to facings at the outer (curved) edges. If you prefer sew-in interfacing, add a narrow hem allowance at facing outer edges. Fold and stitch hem over interfacing edges.

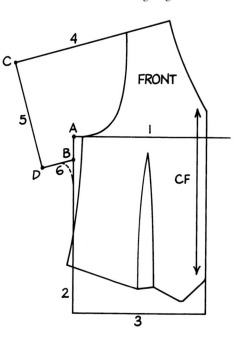

An Elongated Vest

Lengthen the vest to give it added wardrobe importance. Extend the side seamlines downward to the desired finished length. Plan to leave side seams open from about mid-thigh. From this point to the lower edge, add self facings at back and front side seamlines. See the instructions for Pattern A, page 20.

Add front, neck, and armhole facings, or line the entire garment as for the short vest (lining is better with wool or other fabrics that cling).

After adjusting the pattern, lay out the pieces to determine fabric yardage requirements. Remember to add seam and hem allowances when cutting.

For this variation, you might like to stitch the darts slightly narrower at the midsection for an easier fit. Taper lower ends of the darts like the upper ends, and clip toward the stitching at the center.

This versatile linen vest doubles as a sundress in summer, or combines with other pieces to expand the travel wardrobe. For the cooler seasons, make it with heavier fabric and wear it with leggings and sweater, or as a jumper.

A B C D E F G H I

The Big Vest

Make either a vest or a jacket with this versatile pattern. It's cut straight and oversized, roomy enough to wear with a heavy sweater or shirt. The vest pattern adapts well to fabrics too heavy for a more fitted style. Blanket-weight wool, quilted materials, boiled wool, and heavy melton would all make great bodywarmers.

INSTRUCTIONS

Detailed information about working with the patterns is on page 106. For many of the construction steps, additional instructions are given in the Sewing Techniques section that begins on page 111. The pattern is on page 139.

This vest was made of warm wool flannel, lined to the edges and bound with wool foldover braid. To keep the lines fluid, interfacing was not used. Big patch pockets serve as handwarmers.

The vest's simple lines make it a perfect candidate for embellishment. Crewel yarn was used here to add a simple design, worked in soft colors with chain stitch. Pearl cotton or several strands of embroidery floss could be used, too. With soft or unstable fabrics, use a backing such as cotton lawn behind the embroidery to prevent stretching the fabric.

The Big Vest

MATERIALS

Fabric and Lining

45" (115 cm):

　All sizes, 2 yds (1.85 m)

60" (152 cm):

　All sizes, 1 yd (.95 m)

Lay out pattern pieces to determine fabric requirements for fabric widths not given above, if substantial alterations are made, or if fabric has a pattern that must be matched.

Other Materials

- Wool foldover braid. To determine yardage, measure the vest seamline around fronts, neck, and lower edge. Measure armholes and upper edges of pockets. Add several inches for overlaps at ends.
- Basting liquid or fusible web, to secure braid for stitching
- Embroidery floss or crewel wool, if desired, for embellishment

CUTTING

Cut pieces 1 and 2 from garment fabric as shown in the layout diagram. Cut 2 pockets, using the larger patch pocket pattern, page 141. Cut lining pieces the same.

　Cut vest front and back, and front and back lining pieces, without adding seam allowances. For pocket and lining, add seam allowances at sides and lower edge.

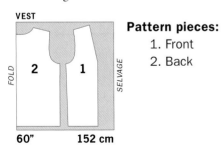

VEST

FOLD　2　1　SELVAGE

60"　152 cm

Pattern pieces:

1. Front
2. Back

CONSTRUCTION

For some of the construction steps below, additional information can be found in the Sewing Techniques section that begins on page 111.

1. Work embroidery on vest front pieces before assembling the vest.

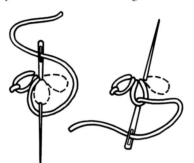

CUSTOMIZE YOUR VEST WITH A SIMPLE CHAIN STITCH DESIGN.

Pockets

2. Stitch pocket to pocket lining at sides and lower edge with right sides together. Trim; turn right side out and press. Baste layers together close to upper edge.

3. Cut strips of braid 1" (3 cm) longer than pocket width. Press under 1/2" (1.5 cm) at each end of a strip. Working on the pocket wrong side, position trim over upper edge with the wider side of the trim to the inside of the pocket. Use basting liquid to hold the braid in place, or press in small pieces of fusible web at intervals. Stitch close to the edge of the braid on the pocket right side.

4. Position pockets on the vest fronts. Baste, then topstitch in place.

Fronts and back

5. Stitch fronts to back at shoulders with right sides together.

6. Stitch together at side seamlines.

7. Assemble lining in the same way.

8. Position lining in vest with wrong sides together.

9. Machine baste lining to vest around outer edges and armholes, stitching close to the edges.

Finishing

10. Beginning at an inconspicuous point, apply braid to vest outer edges and armholes. Turn under ends, or overlap ends and zigzag across the raw edge.

11. Mark and work buttonholes. Stitch on the buttons.

The Big Jacket

Just add sleeves to convert the vest to a warm jacket. Use traditional lining fabric, or try soft cotton flannel in a bright plaid. For dressy occasions, make it of mohair and line it with silk charmeuse.

MATERIALS

Fabric

JACKET AND LINING, ALL SIZES

45" (115 cm):
   2-5/8 yds (2.40 m)

60" (152 cm):
   2 yds (1.85 m)

Lay out pattern pieces to determine fabric requirements for sizes and fabric widths not given above, if substantial alterations are made, or if fabric has a pattern that must be matched.

Other Materials

- Interfacing, 1 yd (.95 m), lightweight fusible knit
- Embroidery floss, crewel yarn, or pearl cotton, for embellishment
- Stabilizer tape for neckline and front yoke seams

CUTTING

Add seam and hem allowances to pieces before cutting.

To add the decorative front yoke, cut across the jacket front pattern piece at about the armhole matching point.

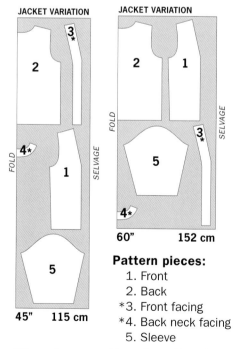

Pattern pieces:
1. Front
2. Back
*3. Front facing
*4. Back neck facing
5. Sleeve

*These pieces are cut from other pattern pieces as described in the cutting instructions.

Make the cut exactly perpendicular to the center front line. Add seam allowances at both cut edges when cutting fabric. Add hem allowance at the lower edge of the lower front piece. Cut two of each piece. (Cut front lining and facing from the original pattern.)

To omit cuffs, cut off 1-5/8 (4 cm) from cuff at lower edge of sleeve; cut lining to hemline.

Cut pieces 2 and 5 according to the layout diagram. Add hem allowance at the lower edge of piece 2 and seam allowance at the lower edge of piece 5.

Cut facings using pieces 1 and 5, adding seam allowances, and hem allowance at the front facing lower edge. Cut interfacing for facings, omitting hem allowance.

Cut lining with pieces 1, 2, and 5. Add seam allowances. Cut pieces 1 and 2 to lower edge hemline, and piece 5 to cutting line indicated on pattern piece. Cut 2 pieces for pocket linings 7" (18 cm) wide and 16" (41 cm) long.

Transfer pattern markings to garment pieces.

CONSTRUCTION

1. Work embroidery on front yoke sections.

Pockets

This pocket style is suitable only for fabrics that do not ravel. A lined patch pocket can be substituted; make it according to the instructions on page 000.

2. Fold and press each end of pocket lining 3/4" (2 cm) to wrong side.

3. Carefully cut jacket lower fronts along pocket slash lines.

4. Center one end of lining at lower edge of pocket slash, wrong side of lining to wrong side of jacket, with lining fold just below pocket edge. Pin. Stitch on the right side 1/4"(7 mm) below pocket edge, taking care not to stretch fabric.

5. Pin other lining fold behind upper pocket edge and stitch in the same way. Crease across the upper lining above the pocket to form the pocket pouch.

6. With pocket edges together, stitch across at the ends for reinforcement.

7. Fold back the jacket and stitch sides of pocket lining together from the upper fold, stitching close to the pocket corners. Trim, and overcast edges if necessary.

8. On the outside, work blanket stitch from the topstitching line over the cut edges of the pocket.

Made in a heavy cotton knit and trimmed with both hand and machine decorative stitching, this oversized lined jacket provides a warm outer layer over sportswear. A front yoke was added just for fun, and embroidery worked above the yoke seam. Blanket stitch provides a distinctive finish at the neckline and front edges, and around the turned-back cuffs. The jacket would make up just as well in almost any cozy fabric: corduroy, wool flannel, denim, or cotton chamois.

Wool gabardine makes an elegant version of the vest, with neat patch pockets for added interest. Team it with matching pants and a simple tee in silky pima cotton, or dressier silk charmeuse, and you have an outfit to draw compliments on many occasions.

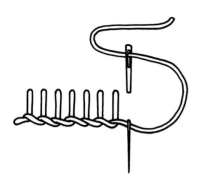

FOR A QUICK AND EASY DECORATIVE FINISH, WORK BLANKET STITCH WITH EMBROIDERY COTTON OR FINE YARN.

Front, back, and facings

9. Sew front yokes to lower fronts with right sides together. For knits, cut a tape stay by the pattern seamline and incorporate into this seam to prevent stretching. Press seam open. On outside, topstitch above seamline. On the jacket shown, a line of machine zigzag stitch was sewn across the yoke with buttonhole thread.

10. Sew fronts to back at shoulders, right sides together.

11. Fuse interfacing to wrong side of facing pieces following manufacturer's instructions.

12. Stitch front facings to back neck facing at shoulders with right sides together.

13. Cut stabilizer tape for front and back neckline, cutting length according to the pattern seamlines.

14. Incorporating tape stay in the seamline, pin facing to jacket, right sides together, around neck and front edges. Stitch. Trim. press seam allow-ances toward facing, then fold facing to inside and press seamline slightly toward facing.

Sleeves and side seams

15. Ease stitch upper sleeves between matching points: Lengthen upper thread tension slightly and stitch on the seamline on the fabric right side. Draw up bobbin threads and ease sleeve to fit armhole, matching markings and shoulders. Stitch.

16. With right sides together, stitch sides and sleeve in a continuous seam.

17. Press hem at jacket lower edge and facings. Fold facings to wrong side along seamline, pin and stitch along hemline fold. Trim; turn right side out.

18. Stitch hem with hand or machine blind stitch.

Lining

19. Sew lining fronts, back, and sleeves as for the jacket. Stay stitch neck edges.

20. Pin lining to jacket facing edges. Stitch, beginning and ending approximately 6" (15 cm) above the jacket lower edge.

21. At the lower edge, match lining edge to edge of jacket hem. Pin, and stitch by hand. A pleat will form across the lower lining. At lining edges, turn under lining seam allowances and finish stitching lining to facings.

22. Press and stitch sleeve hems. Topstitch 1/4" from edges. Attach lining as on jacket hem.

Finishing

23. On the outside, topstitch front and neckline, stitching 1/4" (.7 mm) from edges.

24. Work blanket stitch around front, neckline, and sleeves. Use topstitching as a guide, and stitch just through outer fabric.

25. Mark and work buttonholes. Sew on buttons.

Pockets

Take a plain shirt, add a well-designed pocket, and you've converted an uninteresting garment to one with character. Shirt pockets, visible as they are, should be carefully placed and stitched. Uneven pockets with wobbly topstitching can spoil the look of a garment, yet a nicely made pocket will draw attention from less-than-perfect stitching elsewhere.

Pockets in pants and skirts usually are more functional than decorative, intended to allow hands to enter without a struggle and to keep small objects safely within. Some of us would include pocketless pants in the same category with girdles, plastic shoes, one-size-fits-all pantyhose, body suits, and other articles of clothing designed solely to aggravate.

Patch pockets—those sewn onto the outside of the garment—should be of a size that suits both the garment and the person, not so large as to overwhelm the wearer, nor so small as to look skimpy. Pockets sewn into the garment's side seams, as on skirts and pants, need to be reasonably deep, but not so deep that the fingers can't easily reach to the bottom.

There are entire books devoted just to the design and construction of pockets and the limitless possibilities for creativity they offer. The patterns in this book are the most basic styles, and should serve just as starting points for your own designs. Pocket patterns are on page 141.

PATCH POCKETS

The smaller pattern provided is for the breast pocket on shirt or jacket, and the larger one for the jacket's lower front. There is a flap pattern for each.

Sew pockets to the garment front pieces as the first step in construction. The pocket patterns given here can be shaped as you wish, with the lower corners square or rounded. Use a purchased pocket template, or make one of stiff, lightweight cardboard, to make sure corners are precise and even.

With striped or plaid fabric, the pattern on the pocket should match that of the garment front. With very stable fabric the pockets can be cut on the bias for an interesting effect—and so that matching is unnecessary.

Patch pockets of heavy or stretchy fabrics should be lined. It's best always to line those on the lower front of the garment, which are subject to harder wear. Use the larger pattern for lower pockets, the smaller one for breast pockets.

UNLINED PATCH POCKET

This pocket is suitable for light to medium weight fabrics and is hemmed along the upper edge.

1. Cut the pocket pieces, adding seam allowance at the sides and lower edge. At the top add 1-3/8" (4 cm) hem allowance for a smaller pocket; 1-5/8" (4.5 cm) for the larger size.

2. Fold under upper edge 1-3/8" (4 cm); press. Fold under raw edge 3/8" (1 cm), press, and stitch close to fold on right side.

3. Turn under seam allowances on sides and lower edge; press. For rounded corners, press over the template. If fabric is difficult to press, gather by hand around the corners and draw up the threads to keep corners in place.

4. Miter square corners: Unfold seam allowances at corners and re-fold diagonally across the intersection of the seamline creases; press. Fold in the corners again, and press.

5. Fold and press a tuck in each seam allowance at the top so they won't show above the hemmed edge. Trim raw edges to 1/4" (.5 cm).

6. Carefully position the pockets on the garment. Pin, then baste approximately 1/8" from the edge. Topstitch in place, stitching very close to the edges. If a single row of topstitching will be used, stitch a small triangle at the top of the pocket to reinforce it.

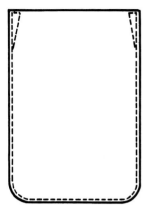

STITCH A TRIANGLE AT EACH UPPER CORNER FOR POCKET SECURITY.

7. For a sturdier and sportier-looking pocket, stitch a second row of topstitching 3/16" (.5 cm) inside the first row. Stitch across the upper edge between the two rows of topstitching.

For a buttoned pocket, work a buttonhole at the center of the pocket hem before sewing the pocket to the garment. Stitch a small scrap of fabric to the wrong side of the garment while sewing on the button to reinforce a lighter weight fabric.

PATCH POCKET WITH FLAP

1. For each pocket, cut two flap sections, adding seam allowance. If the fabric is heavy or if the pocket will be lined, cut one flap section from lining fabric.

2. With lighter fabrics, stitch flap sections, right sides together, at sides and lower shaped edge. With a lined flap of heavy fabric, stitch the upper edge as well, but leave an opening at center for turning. Turn right side out; press.

3. If flap is lined, turn in seam allowances along opening and stitch by hand. Topstitch sides and lower edge as for pocket.

4. For flap of lighter fabric, position wrong side up on garment above the pocket, flap raw edges toward upper edge of pocket and flap seamline 3/4" (2 cm) to 1-1/4" (3 cm) above the pocket edge, depending on the pocket size. Stitch along the seamline. Trim seam allowances evenly.

5. Fold the flap downward; press. Topstitch across flap upper edge.

6. For the lined flap, position right side up, spacing it as above, and topstitch in place.

For a buttoned flap, work the buttonhole before sewing the flap in place. Check flap placement to allow for button to be sewn on the pocket hem.

PLEATED PATCH POCKET

A simple tuck along the front creates a nice design detail with little extra effort.

1. Cut the pattern in half down the center. Move the halves 4" (10 cm) apart, keeping upper and lower edges aligned. Cut the pocket this size, adding seam and hem allowances as above. At the top and bottom edges, mark the center and mark a point 2" (5 cm) each side of center.

2. Fold in half from the wrong side, matching marked points. Stitch down from the upper marked points 2 3/4" (7 cm). Stitch up 5/8" (1.5 cm) from the lower marked points. Press the pleat evenly to each side of center to form a box pleat on the right side.

A SIMPLE POCKET IS ENHANCED BY INTRICATE TOPSTITCHING WITH CONTRASTING THREAD.

A SPORTY POCKET STYLE SUITS THIS CASUAL DRESS.

3. For an inverted pleat, just fold and stitch from the right side.

4. Hem and stitch the pocket as for the plain patch pocket, above.

LINED PATCH POCKET

The addition of lining makes a smoother-looking pocket that will hold its shape. As an alternative to traditional lining fabric, it's fun to use scraps from another project—perhaps a bright silk print for a conservative tweed jacket pocket. The lining fabric should be stable and light in weight.

1. Cut fabric for the outer pocket, adding 1" to 1-1/4" (2.5 cm to 3 cm) hem allowance at the upper edge and seam allowance on all four sides. Cut lining fabric with seam allowances, but omitting the hem allowance.

2. With right sides together, stitch lining to pocket across upper edge seamline leaving an opening approximately 1-1/2" (4 cm) at the center. Press seam allowances toward lining.

3. If the outer fabric is fairly heavy, trim approximately 1/16" (1-2 mm) from the outer edge of the lining so the pocket will curve toward the lining side.

4. With right sides together, pin pocket to lining around lower edges and sides, aligning the edges. Stitch. Trim and grade seam allowances; press. Turn right side out and press.

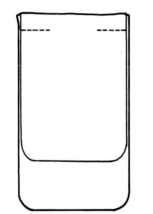

STITCH LINING TO POCKET ACROSS UPPER EDGE, LEAVING THE CENTER OPEN.

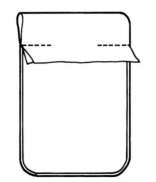

STITCH SIDES AND LOWER EDGE; TURN THROUGH THE OPENING.

5. Baste to the garment and edgestitch in place.

For a dressier look, a lined pocket can be sewn invisibly to the garment. Every fabric combination requires slight adjustments in stitch settings, so practice this technique first with scraps of your fabrics.

Baste the pocket in place, stitching approximately 3/4" (2 cm) from the edge. Set the machine for the blind hem stitch and narrow the stitch width slightly. Use the zigzag presser foot. Carefully fold back the outer fabric and stitch exactly next to the edge of the lining so that the zigzag step of the stitch catches the lining fabric but not the outer fabric. Then press the pocket to cover the stitching.

INSEAM POCKETS

With this style the pocket edges are even with the side seamlines, so the pocket is not highly visible. Since the lining can show when you sit, use a fabric that matches or coordinates with the garment fabric.

On the garment front pattern, pin waistline pleats or darts in place. Adjust side and waistline seams on the inner pocket pattern to match those of the garment. Fit the garment pattern before cutting the pocket pieces so you can change pocket side seamlines and waist seamline accordingly. Mark matching points from the inner pocket pattern onto the garment side seamlines.

To convert a cut-in front pocket to an inseam pocket, as for Pattern G, tape a piece of tracing paper over the pocket area on the front pattern piece. Lay the front pattern over the back pattern piece, matching side seamlines and pocket matching points. Trace the side seamline and waistline from the back pattern to the front.

1. For each pocket, cut two lining sections from the inner pocket pattern, adding standard seam allowances at sides and waist, and a narrow seam allowance at the curved inner edge. Cut a strip of stabilizer tape for each pocket side seamline.

2. With right sides together, sew a lining section to each side of garment back, matching markings and using 1/4" (.5 cm) seam allowance. Sew the companion lining section to the garment fronts in the same way, incorporating a strip of tape into the seam. Press seam allowances toward the lining.

3. Understitch lining to seam allowances, stitching 1/8" (3 mm) from seamlines.

4. Stitch garment side seams above and below markings for pocket opening.

5. Press pocket toward garment front, and press pocket front along side seamline. Clip garment seam allowance as necessary.

6. Inside, stitch lining sections together, using a narrow seam allowance, between side seams. Overcast outer edges.

7. Topstitch front pocket opening, if desired.

8. Stitch darts or pleats in garment front.

9. Baste pocket upper edges in waist seam allowances.

CUT-IN FRONT POCKET

This pocket is most often used for sportswear and gives the garment a casual look. Since the upper back pocket section is visible, that piece is cut from garment fabric. With heavy outer fabric, the piece can be cut from lining, then a facing of the garment stitched over top at the visible area of the pocket.

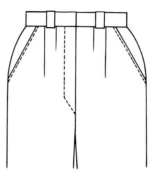

A TAPE STAY SEWN INTO THE POCKET FRONT/LINING SEAM PREVENTS STRETCHING AT THE POCKET EDGE.

Make any fitting adjustments to the garment side and waist seams first, then match the upper and outer edges of the inner pocket pattern to the side and waist seamlines of the garment as for the inseam pocket. Mark pocket opening on side seamlines of garment front and back pattern pieces. Trace the side and waist seamlines onto a piece of paper to start the pocket pattern, or use the pocket pattern as a guide.

If you are adding this pocket to a garment with a different pocket, or no pocket, use the dotted line on the inner pocket pattern piece to mark the upper front corner seamline of the garment front.

1. Cut two lining sections from the inner pocket pattern, using the dotted line as the seamline. Add standard seam allowances at side seamline, diagonal seamline, and upper edges. Add narrow seam allowance at inner curved edges.

2. From garment fabric, cut two pieces the full size of the pattern piece, adding seam allowances as above. These are the back pocket sections.

3. Cut two strips of stabilizer tape the length of the diagonal seamlines.

4. With right sides together, stitch the lining sections to garment fronts at the diagonal seamlines, incorporating the tape into the seam. Press seam allowances toward the lining. Understitch. Fold lining to wrong side along seamline; press. Topstitch the seamed edge if desired.

5. Pin pocket back pieces, right side up, to the wrong sides of garment front. Align pocket outer edges and side seam markings. Stitch pocket sections together around the curved outer edge; overcast.

6. Stitch darts or pleats in garment front.

7. Baste pockets to front at upper edge and side seamline.

8. Stitch garment side seams, treating pocket as one with the garment front.

Embellishments

It takes very little to convert a plain and simple pattern to a garment that's a designer original – with you, of course, as the designer. The embellishment may be as simple as substituting a decorative stitch for straight topstitching, stitching a few ornamental beads onto a pocket flap, adding an embroidered or appliqued motif to the shirt cuffs, or replacing austere buttons down the front of a garment with oversized or mismatched ones.

Elaborate embellishments can be added with any sort of medium. Fabric paints let you create your own "prints". Yarn or threads can be couched onto the fabric to create a pattern. Fabric can be manipulated by folding and stitching intricate patterns of tucks and pleats.

Look everywhere for ideas. Prowl through expensive shops. Clip photos and art from magazines. There are dozens of books featuring copyright-free designs to be found in art and craft supply stores. Wander through craft stores, too, to learn about the new materials available for garment decoration. Keep a notebook to sketch interesting details you notice on other people's clothes, and to jot down ideas that come to you at odd times.

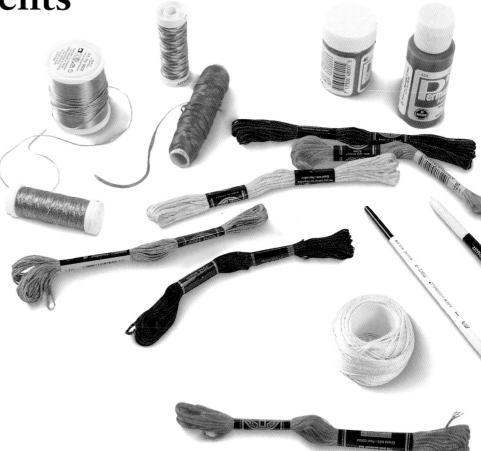

KEEP IN MIND A FEW GUIDELINES WHEN YOU EMBELLISH A GARMENT:

- Make a copy of the pattern piece(s) you plan to decorate and draw your design. Sometimes an idea that's delightful in a small sketch becomes overwhelming when enlarged to life size.

- Practice the technique first on scraps of your garment fabric.

- If possible, work the embellishment on a single garment piece before construction. It's easier to maneuver.

- Designs that involve applique, dense stitching, beading, etc., may require a backing so as not to stretch or pucker the fabric. Use a backing material appropriate for both your fabric and the technique; ask for advice where you buy your supplies.

Many of the garments made from our basic patterns feature small added details that change the finished garments in a big way. Instructions are given for these, but you'll soon have hundreds of your own unique ideas.

Seamlines can be added almost anywhere on a garment to allow you to insert trim, piece fabrics together, or to work lines of topstitching in unexpected places. Draw the proposed cutting lines on a copy of the pattern to help you picture the finished design. And remember to add a seam allowance at each cut edge.

On a camp shirt adapted from Pattern A, what appears to be a great deal of time-consuming handwork is purchased insertion that resembles fagoting. Shops that stock heirloom sewing supplies offer a wide selection of decorative embroidered and lace trims for insertion between fabrics.

The decorative trim used here was finished on both edges. If your choice has unfinished edges, give them a rolled finish with a zigzag stitch set at medium length and width. Then stitch with the garment fabric over the rolled edge.

Tip: Use cotton lingerie weight thread to sew the insertion. Because this thread is finer, the stitching is barely visible and the seam less bulky.

CUTTING

Refer to the cutting instructions for Pattern A, page 20. Lay out the altered pattern pieces to determine fabric yardage needed.

1. Cut across the shirt front pieces where the inserts will be placed, making the cuts exactly perpendicular to the center front (lengthwise grain) line.

2. Make a separate facing. Cut along the pattern facing foldline, adding seam allowance to both shirt and facing at the cut edge.

3. Cut interfacing for fronts and collar. Note: The interfacing will be visible through the insertion. With lightweight fabric, a piece of the garment fabric can be used to interface.

4. For sleeves, cut off approximately 2" (5 cm) above the hemline. Cut a strip of fabric for a hem facing. Use the lower edge of the shirt pattern as a guide to width. In length, cut the piece twice the desired hem width plus twice the seam allowance.

CONSTRUCTION

1. For the front, fold under and press the edges where horizontal cuts were made. Fold each edge by half the width of the insertion strip. Clean finish the edges.

2. Stitch the trim to one shirt section, abutting the trim edge and fold, with a zigzag stitch at medium length and width settings. Sew to the adjacent shirt piece.

3. Fold under a narrow seam allowance at lower edge of sleeve. Press, and clean finish the edge.

4. Fold the sleeve facings in half, right side out, across the width. Turn both seam allowances evenly to the inside and press. Baste folded edges together.

5. Attach the insertion as for the blouse.

6. Follow construction steps on pages 20-24 to complete the blouse.

Fabric paints provide a wonderful means of elevating a simple garment to wearable art. And a vest is the ideal garment of such experimentation—if you decorate just the front (make the back of the same fabric in a solid color, or of lining), you'll be finished before the project can become tiresome.

Several kinds of fabric paints are available, and there are permanent marking pens in every color imaginable. Some require heat setting; some don't. Read the instructions before buying to be sure the product is compatible with your fabric.

Wash the fabric at least once to remove surface finishes that might interfere with paint penetration. Cut out the garment pieces roughly, and lightly pencil in the seamlines to guide your design.

Natural linen becomes a spectacular one-of-a-kind fabric with the application of an all-over embroidered design. The vest is especially striking paired with pants or skirt in the unadorned fabric. This vest was worked by hand in chain stitch with cotton embroidery floss. Machine embroidery can produce a similar effect, as can yarn or fine cord couched onto the fabric. For machine work on lighter weight fabrics, back the fabric with the lightest possible fusible knit interfacing so the fabric won't pucker.

To couch yarn, arrange the strands in the pattern you like, with a drop of basting liquid or spot of fabric glue here and there to hold them in place. Thread the machine with thread to match the yarn, or with invisible thread. Use a cording foot or applique foot, or any presser foot that will move smoothly over the yarn without shifting it. Stitch over the yarn with a medium-length zigzag stitch just wide enough to straddle the yarn strand.

Imaginative tab closures used on both jacket and blouse don't detract from the clothes' simple lines, yet create a look that's far from ordinary. The tabs make up best in a fabric that presses easily, such as linen, shown in the photo, or cotton.

1. For each tab (you need one for each button and each buttonhole), cut a lengthwise strip of fabric 6-1/2" (16.5 cm) long and 1-3/4" (4.5 cm) wide.

2. Fold each end of the strip 1/2" (1.3 mm) to the wrong side; press.

3. Press the strip in half, lengthwise, right side out. Fold raw edges in toward the center for a finished strip width of 1/2" (1.3 mm). Press.

4. Edgestitch the strip along both long edges.

5. Fold the strip in half, aligning the ends, with the double folded edges against each other so that a point forms. Keeping the edges together, stitch across the fold at the base of the point.

6. Position horizontally on the garment with the point almost at the front edge and the base of the point at center front.

7. Stitch the tab to the garment across the straight ends of the tab. For the buttonhole tabs, also stitch from the straight ends approximately 3/4" (2 cm) toward the point on each outer edge, stitching along the previous row of edgestitching. On the button tabs, stitch button at the base of the point, stitching tab to the garment at the same time.

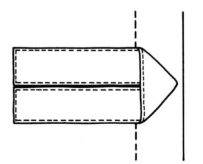

FOLD STRIPS WITH DOUBLE EDGES TOGETHER, PRESS, AND STITCH ACROSS THE BASE OF THE POINT

Stenciling also is done with fabric paint, applied with a special brush. Trace a design onto special template material – it's available, along with the brushes, at craft supply stores. Cut away the design area with a sharp craft knife.

Prepare the fabric, or finished garment, as for painting. Keep the paint fairly thick so it won't flow under the template, and hold the brush in a vertical position to dab on the paint. To work on a finished garment, place a thickness of unprinted newsprint or other clean paper under the area to prevent paint bleeding through to the other fabric layer.

Creating a Wardrobe

Millions of words have been written offering help to women in achieving their dreams of wardrobe perfection, a closet full of grab-and-go ensembles for every occasion, garments that fit perfectly, look fantastic, and can be mixed and matched endlessly. It's a pleasant dream.

Building a great wardrobe really isn't so difficult. There are just three things you have to do: plan, sew, and shop.

PLANNING REQUIRES A LITTLE TIME AND A FIRM WILL.

- Don't buy on impulse (or on sale) anything that isn't on your want list. Ditto for accepting hand-me-overs from friends and sisters.

- Choose a favorite garment or several and work around them, rather than trying to create an outfit based on a garment that should instead be discarded.

- Apply a touch of realism to the planning process. Plan for the way you really live. Tame your desire for floaty silk at least until you can dress yourself for work five days straight. Give up dry-clean-only wool slacks until the kids start school.

- Try, each season, for just one good outfit that can take you almost anywhere.

AS FOR SEWING, FEW OF US, GOOD INTENTIONS NOTWITHSTANDING, HAVE TIME TO MAKE EVERYTHING WE WEAR. APPLY REALISM HERE, TOO.

- Make clothes that are very special. Make one superb jacket that will go with several basic skirts and pants. Make a dress for a momentous occasion.

- Make it if you can't seem to buy one that fits you. Pants often are the culprit. While you might spend a full weekend adjusting a pants pattern, you could spend weeks roaming the malls to find a pair that fits to your satisfaction. Sewing is more fun.

- Sew when you can make the garment for a fraction of the cost of its ready-to-wear counterpart. People think we sew to save money; let's try to sustain the myth.

- Sew when you find an irresistible piece of fabric – and also have a firm plan for its use.

- Sew when you have an uncompromising requirement as to color, fabric, or style. Usually it is easier to find the fabric than the finished garment.

IN THE INTEREST OF CREATING A WARDROBE, SOMETIMES IT'S BETTER *NOT* TO SEW.

- Buy it if the style and quality are to your liking, and the price is right.

- Buy the basics, like jeans and khakis, a navy wool blazer, a black skirt. They're usually not so difficult to find.

- Buy a garment that would be ridiculously time-consuming to make or one that's beyond your current sewing ability. The latter is liable to dull your interest in sewing those things that you can do very well.

USE THE BASIC PATTERNS TO FILL THE GAPS IN YOUR WARDROBE. AND USE THEM TO CREATE WONDERFULLY ORIGINAL CLOTHES THAT EXPRESS YOUR INDIVIDUALITY.

As the suit to take you almost everywhere, this one is tops. Wool crepe makes it a rugged traveler, and it's comfortable in all but the warmest weather. Add a long skirt in the print fabric, another shirt or two, and you're packed for a week away.

Just five pieces, but there is plenty of potential. Shop and sew with a color scheme in mind and a wardrobe will practically assemble itself.

Start with a versatile jacket. This one has character of its own, yet it combines harmoniously with skirts and pants in lots of lengths and colors. With a perfect white shirt and a simple black sweater, you're ready to go.

Basics don't always have to be neutral colors. Use this tropical print for a long, flowing skirt, make shorts or pants in coral, add a bright silky shirt, and all sorts of combinations are possible.

Working with the Patterns

The patterns included here differ in several ways from most commercial patterns. Please read through this section so you will understand how best to prepare and use the patterns—it will save you time in the long run.

HOW THEY DIFFER FROM COMMERCIAL PATTERNS

Multiple sizes are included on each pattern. For those of us whose measurements don't match the charts, it's easy to combine the waistline of one pattern size with the hip of another for a pattern that really fits. And if you need a size smaller or larger than the pattern provides, you can use the existing lines as a guide for creating your size.

Seam allowances are not included. Lines shown on the patterns are hemlines or seamlines rather than cutting lines; seam and hem allowances must be added before or while cutting the pieces. There are several advantages to this system.

Since alterations should be made from seamlines, it is easier to make both fitting and design changes if you don't have to draw in the seamlines first.

You can add just the amount of seam allowance you need, and save time trimming later. For example, 1/4" (.5 cm) is adequate at the outer edges of a collar where no fitting will be necessary, while you may want to add 1" (2.5 cm) at the center back seam of pants to allow for adjustments. For fusible interfacing, it is not necessary to add any seam allowance.

Some of the pattern pieces serve a dual purpose. Pattern pieces marked * on the layout diagrams are actually cut from other pieces. The inner seamline for a front facing, for example, is usually shown on the garment front pattern piece. This allows for cutting facings so they match the garment accurately. It also allows you to cut a lining easily; the facing seamline becomes the outer seamline for the lining piece.

Some pattern pieces are not included. Rectangular pieces, such as waistbands and cuffs, can be cut more quickly and accurately from measurements than with a pattern piece, especially if a rotary cutter is used. Measurements are given with the cutting instructions, and those pieces are marked ** on the layout diagrams.

The chart below shows measurements upon which the pattern sizing is based. Most of the patterns include generous design ease. Measurements are given in inches with equivalents in centimeters below, in parentheses.

Pattern Size	XXS	XS	S	MS	M	ML	L	XL
Approximate Ready-to-Wear Equivalent	6	8	10	12	14	16	18	20
Bust	31 (78.5)	32 (81)	33 (84)	34-1/2 (87.5)	36-1/2 (92.5)	38-1/2 (97.5)	40 (101.5)	42 (106.5)
Waist	24 (61)	25 (63.5)	26 (66)	27 (68.5)	28-1/2 (72.5)	30 (76)	31-1/2 (80)	33 (83/5)
Hips	34 (86)	35 (89)	36 (91.5)	37-1/2 (95)	39-1/2 (100)	41 (104)	42-1/2 (108)	44 (111.5)

COPYING THE PATTERNS

The pattern pieces shown on the book pages are 25 percent of actual size. A good photocopy shop can enlarge them for you. Take care piecing the enlargements; compare the lines to the original pattern illustration.

An alternative is to copy the pattern by hand, drawing it at actual size onto pattern drafting material printed with a one-inch grid (available from notions suppliers). Make sure to transfer all matching points accurately.

Keep your full-size pattern pristine. Trace a copy of it for fitting purposes and to experiment with design changes.

PATTERN SIZING

As is well known by any woman who has ever bought or sewn a garment, there is no such thing as standard sizing in women's clothes. What constitutes perfect fit is somewhat arbitrary, too; some of us prefer a sleek fit to our clothes, while others of us prefer garments that are rather roomy.

Most of the patterns in this book include a moderate to considerable amount of design ease. The exceptions are pants, and waistbands of skirts. The size chart should be used just as a guide. Measurements should be checked against other garments, and test garments should be made if you are unsure of the amount of ease that suits you. Measurements are given in inches with equivalents in centimeters shown in parentheses.

HOW TO READ THE PATTERNS

On each pattern a different line style is used for each of the sizes given. Solid lines are seam or hemlines common to all sizes. Interior lines, such as facing seamlines, are shown as finer solid lines. Until you're used to working with this system, you might wish to highlight the lines for your size with a marker so you will see them easily.

Matching points, shown as solid diamond-shaped symbols on most commercial patterns, are indicated on these patterns by short straight lines perpendicular to the seamlines. Just extend these lines to your marked cutting line, then cut them as traditional notches outside the cutting line, or mark with fabric marker.

FABRIC YARDAGE REQUIREMENTS

Yardage information given with the pattern instructions is for the most commonly used fabric widths, and for the largest and smallest of the pattern size range. Yardages allow for one-directional layout of pattern pieces, so there is no need to adjust for fabrics with nap or one-way designs. Allowance is made for minor shrinkage only; for fabrics such as knits that can shrink considerably, it is wise to buy extra yardage. It will also be necessary to buy extra for matching plaids or prints.

If major alterations are made, in length especially, or if changes or additions are made to the design, be sure to lay out the pattern pieces to determine yardage needs. A gridded cardboard cutting mat is very helpful for this task.

Beware of using a yardage conversion chart for this purpose. These give the equivalent square inches for fabrics of different widths, but cannot indicate whether there will be sufficient length for your pattern pieces.

FITTING THE PATTERNS

There are excellent books on the subject of pattern fitting. If you have chronic difficulties in this area, it is a good idea to study one of them.

When you measure in preparation to making pattern adjustments, be sure to consider what will be worn under the new garment. For an outerwear jacket, measure over a heavy sweater or shirt; for a waistband, wear whatever will tuck into it.

A good first step toward making a garment that fits is to measure a similar one whose fit you like. This will give you an idea of the amount of ease you prefer. Compare your own measurements at key points to those of the garment, then check the results against the pattern.

PATTERN CHANGES

Always use the lengthwise grainline on the pattern as the constant. Cuts and pleats should be made either parallel or exactly perpendicular to it. Use a carpenter's square for accuracy.

To shorten a pattern piece, fold a pleat across the width. The pleat depth should be half the total change needed. To lengthen, cut the pattern apart and add a strip of paper between the cuts. Arrange the pattern pieces to keep the lengthwise grainline perfectly straight. Then blend the side seamlines smoothly.

MAKING A TEST GARMENT

With any untried pattern, the best way to assure a good fit is to make a test garment, or "muslin", of inexpensive fabric. You can match pattern measurements to your own forever and still not have a true idea of what the garment will look like on you.

This need not be a time-consuming process. Measure yourself against the pattern as a starting point, then cut the main garment pieces from muslin, or for a jacket, from inexpensive fabric in a heavier weight. You won't need facings or collars, or to add hem allow-ances. Do add extra seam allowance where seams may need letting out: at sides, pants crotch, etc. Machine-baste the main seams to try it on. Use shoulder pads if the garment will have them; they affect the fit at shoulders and underarms.

Fitting is much easier with a friend's help. Pin tucks, rip seams, and mark your changes directly onto the muslin. Stitch the adjustments until you're satisfied, then transfer the markings to your pattern. You may find that you don't need to alter the pattern at all, but need simply to use another size.

FITTING TIPS

Most of us need to make one or two adjustments to any pattern we use. Below are suggestions for dealing with the most common of these.

CIRCUMFERENCE

For a top, the starting point is the bust measurement, then you need to know your preference for ease. Measure the pattern front from the center front line, not outer edges. Measure the back. Compare pattern to your desired garment measurement.

WAIST LENGTH

Measure from the nape of your neck to the back waistline. For a shirt that will be tucked in, or a dress worn with a belt, allow an inch or two (3-5 cm) ease for blousing. Adjust the pattern pieces with horizontal pleats or extensions.

SLEEVE LENGTH

Bend your arm slightly and hold your hand in front of you. Have a partner measure from the nape of your neck to the point of your shoulder, down and under your elbow, to your wrist bone. Then arrange the back, sleeve, and cuff patterns to compare. For a shirt sleeve, length usually can be adjusted with one cut or pleat. For a jacket, which has a shaped sleeve, the adjustment may need to be either above or below the elbow, or at both points.

WAISTBANDS

It is a good idea to make the skirt or pants waistband before you sew the rest of the garment so you can fit accurately at the waistline. Measure your waist over a blouse or sweater if you wear them tucked in – and allow a little ease so it will be comfortable after lunch too. Add for overlap at the closures.

PANTS AND SKIRT LENGTH

Adjustments can be made at the hemline unless the length difference is significant, then pleat or cut as for other length alterations. When you measure for pants length, wear the shoe heel height you intend to wear with the garment.

PANTS

Since pants must fit rather closely, and since we are all built differently in this region, a pants pattern may require more manipulation than an oversized shirt, for example. Always make a test garment from a new pants pattern. Once the pattern fits, though, it can be used for years. Some of the most common fitting problems are not difficult to solve.

Cut the test garment with wider seam allowances at side seams and center back and front. When you fit it,

don't put it on wrong side out even though it's easier to mark this way. Most of us are not precisely the same on both sides.

Check the crotch length. Lengthen if pants bind when you're seated, and shorten if they grab at thigh fronts as you walk. Lengthen or shorten with a horizontal pleat or cut about 7" (18 cm) below the waist.

If the seat is baggy or tight and side seams are in the right place, adjust at center back. Adjust for tummy at center front. If pants are loose, or tight, all the way around, make slight adjustments at the side seams or try another pattern size.

Side seams should be correctly located, and should follow the hip contours smoothly. It the side seamlines are changed, remember to make the same adjustments to pocket pieces.

Mark the waistline on the test garment and press under seam allowances on the waistband. Try the band over the pants. Minor differences in hip height can be accommodated at the seamline. If one hip is considerably higher, raise the waistline on that side and adjust the side seamline accordingly. Blend with the original waistline at back and front

Excess fabric just below the waistband in back is a common problem with both pants and skirts. It can usually be corrected by lowering the waistline at center back, blending the seamline to the original at the sides.

ADDING SEAM AND HEM ALLOWANCES

There are several techniques for adding seam and hem allowances to patterns before you cut, and a range of tools available to simplify the process. The method you use will depend to some extent on the fabric with which you're working, but will usually be a matter of personal preference. Experiment to find the one you like. Remember to test any colored marking materials on scraps of your fabric.

A good standard seam allowance is 1/2" to 5/8" (1.5 cm) wide. You can vary it as you wish, but make note of the system you've used unless you mark every seamline as well.

If this is your first experience with patterns of this kind, you may wish to trace the pattern pieces, pencil in cutting lines, cut them out, then cut your fabric. This is a safe way to go, but takes longer than some of the alternatives given below.

Dressmaker's carbon and a tracing wheel are traditional tools for this job. Mark the wrong side of the fabric. Place a see-through ruler along the seamline to add the desired amount of seam allowance, and run the wheel along the ruler's edge. You can mark one thickness of fabric and cut through both layers. Then transfer pattern markings to one piece at a time. With a double tracing you can mark seamline and cutting line at the same time.

A flexible tape measure 5/8" (1.5 cm) wide is also is a handy tool to employ. Mark the garment seamlines as above, then place the tape alongside and mark the cutting lines.

For rotary cutting, there is a cutter available that has a built-in guide. Move the guide along the pattern seamline as you cut.

There are double chalk wheels available, too, that mark seam and cutting lines simultaneously. Then you can cut with scissors or wheel, as you prefer.

Hems should be added to the pattern piece itself before you begin to cut. The process is described in the Sewing Techniques section, page 114.

TRANSFERRING PATTERN MARKINGS

The method you use to mark important points on the garment pieces will usually correspond with the system you use for marking seam allowances, but will also depend upon your fabric.

Always test marking pens or chalks on fabric scraps. Make sure ironing over them won't set the marks. Even when you're reasonably certain of the product's compatibility with your fabric, it's best to mark on the wrong side.

When the texture or pattern of the fabric conceals the work of every marking tool in your kit, remember tailor's tacks. Marking with thread is always the safest and most visible method.

Skilled sewers know that using the correct tool for each sewing procedure not only improves the results, but makes the process more pleasurable. With essential equipment – sewing machine, iron, shears, and pins – always buy the very best quality you can afford. Add the specialized gadgets and accessories as your projects call for them.

Sewing Techniques

In this section are special tips and techniques to supplement the pattern sewing instructions. Space doesn't permit describing all the alternative methods for each technique – a good generic sewing book will do that – but beginning sewers can find detailed instructions for help in making up the garments shown, and experts may find some helpful new tips.

TEN GOOD RULES TO TRY TO FOLLOW

1. Use the best tools you can afford. Sharp scissors and pins, a good readable tape measure, and the right size needles contribute to the enjoyment of sewing by reducing the frustration.

2. Start every project with your machine clean, oiled, and equipped with a new needle.

3. Preshrink your fabrics. Always.

4. Pin seams with pins perpendicular to the seamline and remove each one as you get to it. Sewing over pins not only can break a needle, but may damage the bobbin hook (expensive!) or feed dog teeth, and can throw the needle bar out of alignment.

5. Hold thread ends taut as you begin to stitch.

6. Stitch with the grain of the fabric. Generally this means from the wider part of the piece to the narrower: from bottom to top of a skirt or shirt, from armhole to neckline on shoulder seams.

7. With lightweight fabrics especially, instead of backstitching at the beginning and end of a seam, use a very short stitch length for the first and last 1/2" (1.5 cm) or so.

8. So that the stitches will merge with the cloth, press every line of stitching before pressing a seam open or to the side. Press every seam before sewing across it.

9. To prevent bulky seams, grade the seam allowances. Trim each layer of seam allowance separately so that the one next to the outer garment is widest, and the narrowest layer is to the inside. Trim closely at corners.

10. Never start a project after 9 p.m.

FRONT ROW, LEFT TO RIGHT: folding cardboard cutting mat with printed grid, bias tape maker, seam ripper and buttonhole cutter, loop turner, tube turner, beeswax, specialized presser feet, spring-return tape measure, liquid fray retardant, hand sewing needles, fabric pleater. **CENTER ROW:** embroidery hoop, pin cushion, magnetic pin holder, tracing wheel and dressmaker's carbon, fabric marking pens, chalk markers, point turner, sewing and hemming gauge, glue stick, trimming scissors, sleeve board. **TOP ROW:** clapper and point presser, pressing ham, pocket template, see-through ruler, pinking shears, dressmaker's shears, rotary cutter and gridded cutting mat.

BASTING

No one likes to do it. It is, however, quicker and less painful to hand baste a seam than to rip it out and resew. Take time to baste sections where precise fit is critical, such as on collars and jacket sleeves. Basting is a good idea, too, when less-than-perfect stitching will be highly visible and could ruin the look of the garment, such as on shirt pockets. Slippery fabrics often require basting, as do bias-cut pieces and patterns that must be matched accurately.

Hand basting done with fine, all-cotton thread made especially for the purpose is easiest to remove. Cotton embroidery floss is a good substitute. Silk thread is the best choice if the basted stitches will be pressed because it won't mark the fabric.

BELT CARRIERS

Not only practical for keeping a belt in its place, carriers add a finished look to the skirt or pants. These are 3/8" (1 cm) wide, finished, and fit a 1-1/4" (3.2 cm) waistband.

1. Cut a lengthwise strip of fabric 14" (36 cm) long and 1-1/4" (3 cm) wide. Measurements include seam allowances.

2. Fold strip in half lengthwise, right side out; press. Fold raw edges in to center; press. Stitch close to both edges.

3. Cut the strip into 5 segments, each 1-3/4" (4.5 cm) long.

4. Pin carriers to garment waist, an end aligned with upper edge. Place one between each pair of front pleats, one at each back dart, and one at center back. Baste.

SEW BELT CARRIERS INTO WAISTBAND SEAM ON THE RIGHT SIDE.

5. Sew on the waistband. Topstitch, if desired, keeping the carrier ends free.

6. Turn under 1/2" (1 cm) on carrier ends and pin to band so that folds are even with upper edge of band. Check that belt will slide easily through carriers, but that they are not too loose. Adjust and trim unfinished ends slightly, if necessary.

7. Slipping machine presser foot under loop of carrier, zigzag stitch the end securely in place.

BUTTONED TAB CARRIERS

Try these as a more decorative alternative to the standard carriers. They fit a waistband 1-1/4" (3.2 cm) wide; adjust length for a wider or narrower band.

1. For each tab, cut two pieces of fabric 2-5/8" (6.5 cm) long and 1-1/4" (3 cm) wide, seam allowances included. Cut one of the pieces from lining fabric if outer fabric is bulky.

2. Stitch the pieces with right sides together along the long edges and to a point at one end, using 1/4" (.5 cm) seam allowance. Trim, turn right side out, and press. Edgestitch the finished edges.

3. Position tabs on the finished waistband. Place the unfinished ends on the inside of the band; the tab end will fold over the top to the right side. Stitch the unfinished ends in place with a zigzag stitch to overcast end at the same time.

4. Fold the tabs over the band, points just below the band lower edge. Stitch a button at the end of each, sewing through the tab and the garment.

BUTTONHOLES AND BUTTONS

They are the nemesis of many sewers with good reason: Unattractive buttonholes can spoil the look of an otherwise lovely garment. By following a few guidelines you can increase your buttonhole success rate.

• Mark buttonhole positions carefully. Arrange the buttons at the markings to double check.

• Always use interfacing under buttonholes to prevent puckering.

• Match thread to the fabric, or use a shade slightly darker. Lighter thread for buttonholes cheapens the garment.

• Always make a sample first, using exactly the fabrics and number of layers as in the garment itself. Cut the sample open to make sure the button fits through it just right.

• Adjust the stitch length, even with an "automatic" buttonholer, if necessary. Stitches should be close together, but not so close that the buttonhole is stiff or that stitching distorts the fabric.

- Cut carefully! Insert cutter at one end, cut to the center, then cut from the other end. The cutter should be very sharp; replace it when you find yourself having to saw through the fabric.

- For thick fabrics such as wool tweed, try corded buttonholes. They are both attractive and durable.

- If there is a glare of white interfacing at the buttonhole edges, touch up with a permanent fabric marker to match the garment.

BUTTON AND BUTTONHOLE PLACEMENT

Buttonholes are usually worked in a vertical line on shirts and blouses, dresses, and down skirt fronts. On jackets and on waistbands they are horizontal.

Vertical buttonholes are placed along on the center front (or back) line. On a shirt, the top button should usually be about 1/2" (1.5 cm) from the top. There should be a button even with the bust line. Then space the others evenly. Try to avoid placing a button exactly under the waistband. If very large or rounded buttons are used, substitute smaller, flatter buttons at and below the waist to prevent odd bulges.

On a skirt front, arrange so there is a button at the tummy line. It isn't necessary to continue buttons below the knees unless it's a design decision.

Horizontal buttonholes on a jacket are positioned so that the buttons will be at center front, which means extending the buttonhole about 1/8" (.5 cm) beyond the center line toward the edge.

SEWING ON BUTTONS

Make them secure the first time around and never have to replace them. A sew-through button—one without a shank—should be sewed with a thread shank equal in length to the thickness of the garment front. Use match sticks, fine knitting needles, or some other gadgetry to keep button the correct distance from the garment as you stitch it. On the last stitch, bring the needle down through the button and wrap thread tightly around the previous stitches to form a stem. Stitch to the wrong side and take several back stitches to secure the thread.

CLEAN FINISH

This term simply means to neaten a fabric edge. It can be serged, overcast by hand or machine, pinked, or turned under and stitched if a hem allowance was added. Tricot seam binding can be zigzag stitched over a raw edge for an especially nice finish that doesn't add bulk.

CUFFS - SEE HEMS

DARTS

Mark dart stitching lines as solid lines on the garment piece. Bring lines together on the wrong side and pin. Stitch, starting at the widest point. About 1/2" (1.5 cm) from the point of the dart, shorten the stitch length to a very short setting and sew to the end of the dart. Sew several stitches beyond the edge of the fabric. Tie a tailor's knot but leave fairly long thread tails. Press darts over a ham to maintain the curved shaping.

ELASTIC

There is an elastic made to order for almost any sewing project. Many of the newer kinds are very easy to apply, and are sturdy enough to last the life of the garment. Sports elastic, made for waistbands of pants and shorts, consists of elastic bands with non-elastic stitching lanes in between. With flat-sewn elastics the band is sewn to the fabric without stretching, then its elastic threads drawn up to fit the waist. A caution: the band itself stretches very little, so must be cut long enough to reach around the hips on a garment without a waistline opening.

Conventional elastic suffers in the sewing process; it is weakened each time the needle pierces an elastic strand. It should be sewn with a ball-point needle, and with as little stitching as possible. It is better to thread this elastic into a casing and stitch just across the ends.

HEMS

A hem is a deceptively simple procedure. If nicely sewn it's never noticed; if it is puckered or uneven, it detracts from otherwise fine workmanship. The hem is usually sewn when you're in a hurry to finish the garment, but try to be patient with it.

ADDING HEMS AND CUFFS

When you add a hem or cuff at the lower edge of a sleeve or pants leg, remember the hem and cuff seamlines must mirror those of the side seams. Here's how to do it.

1. To add a hem, trace the lower part of the sleeve or leg, leaving plenty of paper around the edges.

2. Draw a line below the hem and exactly parallel to it. The distance of the new line from the hemline will be the depth of the hem.

3. Fold the paper up along the hemline. Now trace the side seamlines onto each side of the new hem. Add 1/2" (1 cm) below the edge of the hem to turn under if hem edge won't be clean finished or bound.

A cuff is added in the same way, folding the paper as you would fold the sleeve or pants leg to make a cuff.

1. Trace the lower end of the sleeve or leg.

2. Draw a line parallel to the hem. The distance from the hem will be the depth of the cuff.

3. Crease the pattern and fold it upward along the original hem line. Crease along the cuff line and fold downward. Trace the original hem onto the upper layer of paper. This will be the hem line for the cuff. Now fold the paper under the tracing along the cuff hem. Draw a parallel line across the back to represent the edge of the leg or sleeve. It should not extend above the upper edge of the cuff.

4. Trace side seamlines onto cuff and hem.

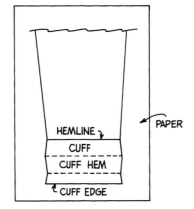

TO ADD A CUFF, FOLD THE PATTERN AS THE HEM AND CUFF WILL BE FOLDED, THEN TRIM ON SIDE SEAMLINES.

HEMMING TIPS

• If you need to adjust the hem width in order for your garments to hang straight, bribe a friend to pin for you, using a yardstick to measure up from the floor.

• Hem stitching should be in keeping with the overall look of the garment. Straight-stitched machine hems are appropriate for sportswear, casual skirts, and for most blouses. Wool pants and skirts, silk tunics, and dressier garments look best with hand- or machine-sewn blind hems. (Master your machine's blind hemmer; it will save you hours of time in the long run.)

• Press the hem in place before clean-finishing the edge to ensure accurate measuring.

• If the hem edge has too much fullness to ease in while pressing, trim off some of the hem allowance. Press the foldline, but press the edge as gently as possible to avoid an imprint on the right side of the garment. It helps to slip a strip of brown kraft paper under the hem edge while pressing.

INTERFACING

Kinds of interfacings are described on page 17.

LINING

A lined garment hangs better, wrinkles less, and keeps its shape for a longer time. The investment of a little extra time during the construction process will pay off with a garment of far better quality. Adding a lining is not the least bit difficult. Lining materials are discussed in the section on fabrics, page 16.

MAKING A JACKET LINING

It's easy to make a lining pattern from the jacket pattern pieces. Use the front, back, and sleeve patterns.

For the front, trace the front pattern piece, using the facing line as the outer seamline. Add seam allowance at this line and at shoulder. Raise the underarm seamline by 1/2" (1.2 cm) to accommodate the jacket underarm seam allowances. Taper to the original seamline at the front matching point. Add seam allowance. At the lower edge, use the jacket hemline as the lining cutting line.

For the back, use the back neck facing line as the upper seamline, and add seam allowance there and at the shoulder. Alter the underarm as for the front. Use the jacket hemline as the lining cutting line. When cutting the back piece, place the center back of the pattern piece 1" (2.5 cm) inside the fabric fold in order to cut the back wider to allow for a pleat.

Alter the underarm at both sides of the sleeve to match jacket front and back alterations. Use jacket sleeve hemline as lining cutting line.

LINING PANTS

Remember the pants lining is actually worn wrong side out. If you have made adjustments on just one side of the pattern, reverse them for the lining.

Cut lining from the garment front and back pattern pieces. If the garment has cut-in pockets, match the side seamline of the lining front to the side seamline of the back pattern piece. Add only a seam allowance at center front; omit the fly extension. Cut front and back to the pants hemline.

1. Construct pants according to the instructions up to the point of attaching the waistband, but don't baste pocket tops at the waistline.

2. Stitch darts and pleats in lining pieces. Press them in the opposite direction of those in the pants.

3. Stitch lining seams. Leave side seams open from approximately 1" (2.5 cm) below pocket openings, and leave center front seam open from 1" (2.5 cm) below lower end of zipper. Press these seam allowances to the wrong side.

4. Slip the lining into the pants. Baste at the waist, matching seams, darts, and pleats. Baste tops of pockets.

5. Attach the waistband.

6. Stitch pressed seam allowances by hand around pockets and zipper openings.

7. Stitch narrow hems in the lining.

SKIRT LININGS

The procedure for lining a straight skirt is the same as for lining pants. For a full skirt, change just a few steps.

With lightweight fabric, baste the lining to the skirt at the waistline before forming the pleats. For heavy fabrics, pleat the skirt separately. Then pleat the lining and press the pleats in the opposite direction. To further reduce waistline bulk, darts can be substituted for pleats in the lining.

For a skirt that buttons down the front, cut the lining to the front facing line, adding seam allowance to both lining and facing. Before attaching the waistband, stitch lining to facing at the facing seamline, stopping about 6" (15 cm) above the hemline. After hemming both layers, finish the seam by hand.

PLAIDS . . .
AND MATCHING THEM UP

The very prospect is enough to keep you from buying that fabric, isn't it? It's not such a difficult job after all, and can be simpler still if you start before you buy the fabric. Select an even plaid, one that "reads" the same from right to left as from left to right. Buy only woven plaid fabric, not one that's printed (the wrong side will look much the same as the right). Unless it is printed exactly with the fabric grain, it will be impossible to match.

Because matching must be done at the seamlines rather than at cutting lines, plaids are easier to match using pattern pieces without the seam allowances on them. Mark placement of seamlines first, then add the cutting lines. It is best to cut pieces individually rather than from doubled fabric.

Match the pattern across the garment front, centering the pattern at center front. Match at the side seams. Match pockets to the pattern at their placement points. Match sleeve seams, at the lower end if the seamlines are

unequal in length as jacket sleeves often are.

Match the sleeve to the garment front, concentrating on the area just above the matching points. With many patterns it won't be possible to match the back of the sleeve as well as the front; this is acceptable.

Unless the fabric is very stable, it is a good idea to baste the seams to keep them matched up perfectly. To do this, position the garments with right sides together. Fold back one seam allowance along the seamline and stitch with a long zigzag stitch, barely catching the fold, with most of the stitch width on the single fabric thickness. Then press the seam allowances together again and stitch the seam. Usually the basting won't show and can be left in place. A walking or even-feed foot also is useful for keeping plaids in line.

PRESSING TECHNIQUES

Pressing well during construction is as important to the results as is the sewing itself. Equip yourself with a top-quality iron and all the pressing aids you can afford; it will make a big difference.

Every fabric differs in its pressing requirements. Test yours to determine the correct iron temperature, how much steam is needed, whether it will be necessary to press only on the wrong side, whether a pressing cloth is necessary, and whether a pounder should be used to flatten seams. Check that your pressing technique won't leave seam allowance imprints on the right side of the garment. If this happens, center the seam along a piece of thick wooden dowel, then press just the stitching line.

After you stitch a seam, press the stitching line to blend stitches with the fabric, then press the seam open or to one side. Press flat seams on a flat surface; curved ones over a ham.

SEAMS AND SEAM FINISHES

The ordinary *straight stitched seam* will serve best in the majority of sewing situations. Adjust the stitch length to suit your fabric, shortening it slightly if the seam puckers. The seam can be finished in a number of different ways (see below).

Most machines now are equipped with a selection of overcast stitches. Each has a particular use, described in your machine manual. Except for sewing knits (see page 37), these stitches are most often used for overcasting seam allowances and for decorative work.

With a *French seam*, raw edges are enclosed. It is a good choice for very sheer fabrics and when the wrong side of the garment can be visible, such as on an overshirt. It is most successful on straight or slightly curved seams. To make a French seam with 5/8" (1.5 cm) seam allowance added:

1. Stitch edges with *wrong* sides together, using 1/4" (.5 cm) seam allowance. Press seam allowances to one side and trim to half the width.

2. Fold along the seamline with right sides together; press.

3. Stitch again, 3/8" (1 cm) from the fold.

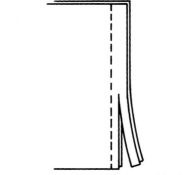

FOR A FRENCH SEAM, FIRST SEW WRONG SIDES TOGETHER AND TRIM SEAM ALLOWANCES.

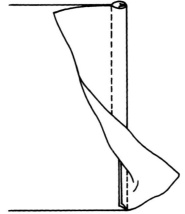

SEW WITH RIGHT SIDES TOGETHER, ENCLOSING THE RAW EDGES.

A *flat-fell seam* also leaves no raw edges. It is a strong seam, often used on tailored shirts and garments that will see a lot of wear. It too works best on seams that are straight or nearly so. Use 1/2" to 5/8" (1.5 cm) seam allowance.

1. Stitch a straight seam with *wrong* sides together, using the full seam allowance. Press to one side.

2. Trim the under seam allowance to half its width.

3. Fold the upper seam allowance around and under the trimmed one, to

the stitching line. Press, and stitch again close to the folded edge.

FINISHING SEAMS

Seams should be finished only enough to prevent raveling. Too much stitching on the inside can leave an imprint on the outside of the garment when it's pressed.

The kind of finish used depends to some extent on the way the seam allowances are pressed. Seams should be pressed open only on garments that will be dry cleaned, otherwise they will have to be pressed open again each time the garment is washed. In this case, trimming with pinking shears is the best finishing method. On medium to heavy fabrics a multiple-step zigzag stitch also will work, but most other overcast stitches will be too dense for the single fabric layer. For fabrics likely to ravel badly, bind each edge with tricot seam binding.

A serger is ideal for most seam finishing, if you're lucky enough to have one. Keep the looper tension adjusted so the edges lie flat.

Overcast stitches can accomplish almost the same thing when seam allowances are pressed in the same direction then trimmed slightly.

A simple zigzag stitch is usually the last choice. It often creates a ridge which will mark the outside of the garment.

TRIMMING AND GRADING SEAM ALLOWANCES

Except for straight seams on lightweight fabrics, seam allowances should be trimmed individually to layer them, which prevents a ridge that will show through to the right side of the garment. Cut the least from the layer next to the garment, the most from the inner layer.

Trim corners close to the stitching, angling the cut toward the corner, so there will be no bulk to round the corner. When close trimming is necessary, as on collar points, use a drop of fray retardant for security.

On curved seams, clip through the seam allowances at intervals so the seamline will lie flat. On outward curves, such as those on a vest's front points, cut notches from the seam allowance to reduce bulk.

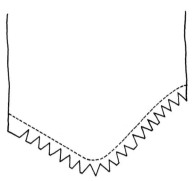

ON CONVEX CURVES, CLIP NOTCHES FROM THE SEAM ALLOWANCE TO REDUCE BULK WHEN THE SEAM IS TURNED.

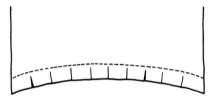

TRIM A CURVED SEAM ALMOST TO THE STITCHING LINE SO IT WILL LIE FLAT.

TOPSTITCHING AND EDGESTITCHING

Topstitching gives a professional finish to many garments, and is functional besides. It keeps facings to the inside of the garment, and it holds interfacings in place.

Topstitching is traditionally worked a scant 1/4" (.5 cm) from the edge; if the stitching is as close as possible to the edge, it's called edgestitching. On tailored shirts and sportswear there is often a line of each. Study good quality ready-to-wear garments to see what topstitching can do.

On thick or fuzzy fabrics, heavier thread might be needed so that the stitching will show. Usually it is available in a limited color range, but two strands of regular thread, sewn with a topstitching needle, will produce the same effect.

Tip: For straight topstitching, don't watch the needle, but look at a point slightly ahead of it. It's just like driving a car: to keep it traveling in a straight line, you look ahead, not at the car's hood ornament.

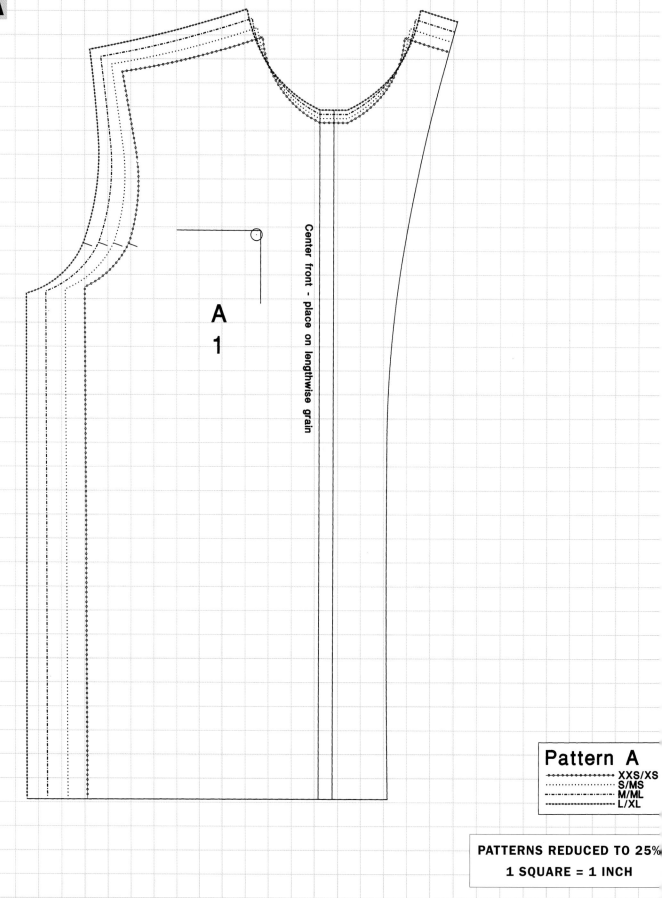

Center front - place on lengthwise grain

A
1

Pattern A

••••••••••	**XXS/XS**
··············	**S/MS**
—·—·—·—	**M/ML**
————————	**L/XL**

PATTERNS REDUCED TO 25%
1 SQUARE = 1 INCH

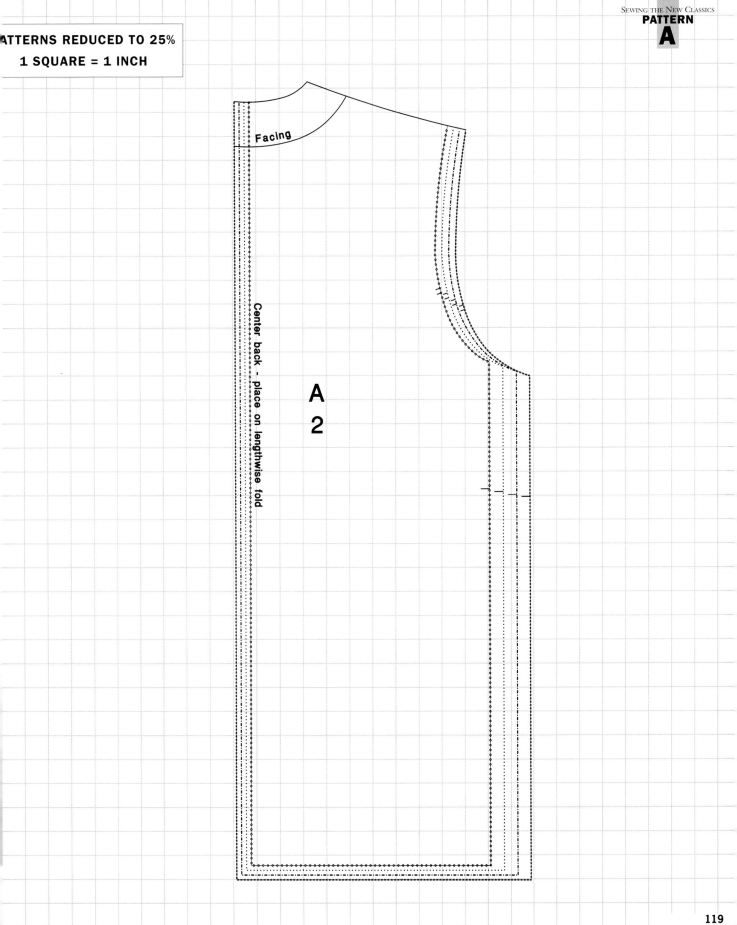

PATTERNS REDUCED TO 25%
1 SQUARE = 1 INCH

Facing

Center back - place on lengthwise fold

A
2

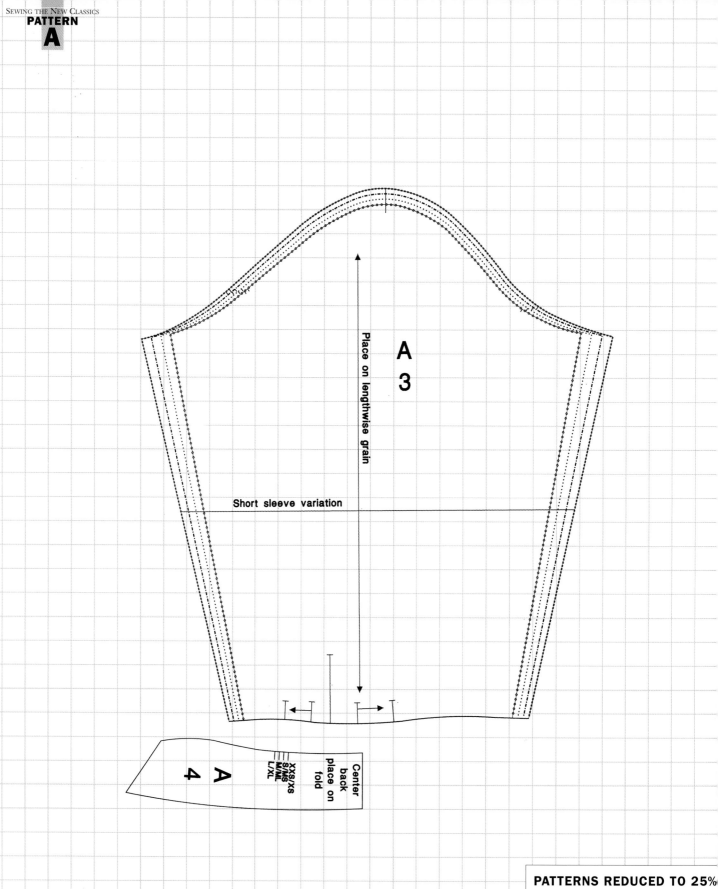

Place on lengthwise grain

A
3

Short sleeve variation

A
4

Center
back
place on
fold

XXS/XS
S/MS
M/ML
L/XL

PATTERNS REDUCED TO 25%
1 SQUARE = 1 INCH

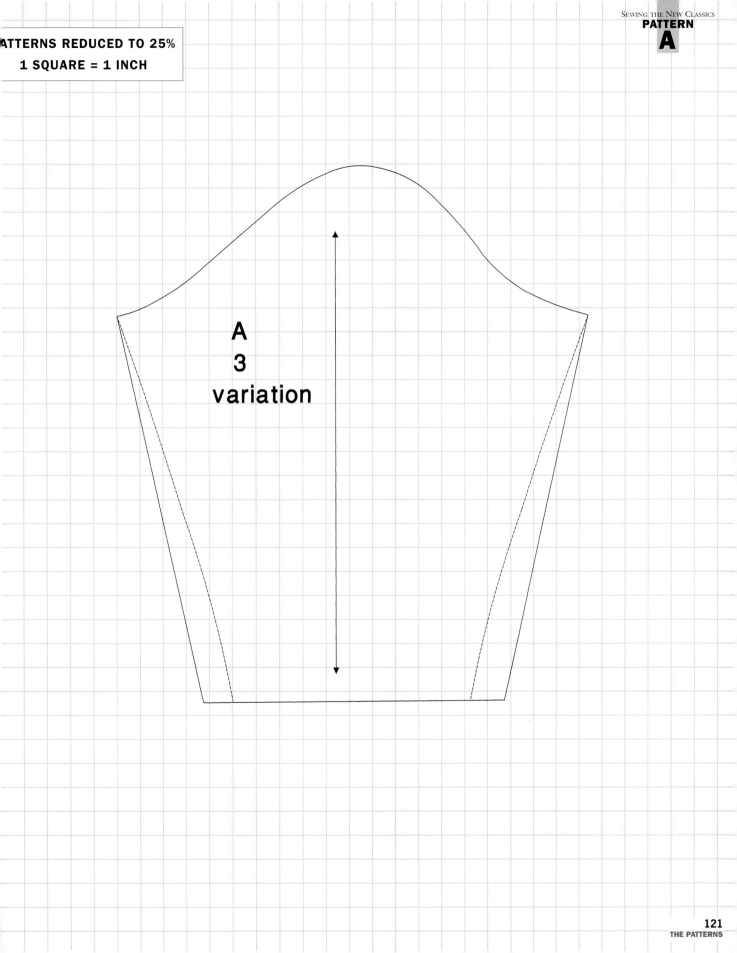

PATTERNS REDUCED TO 25%
1 SQUARE = 1 INCH

A
3
variation

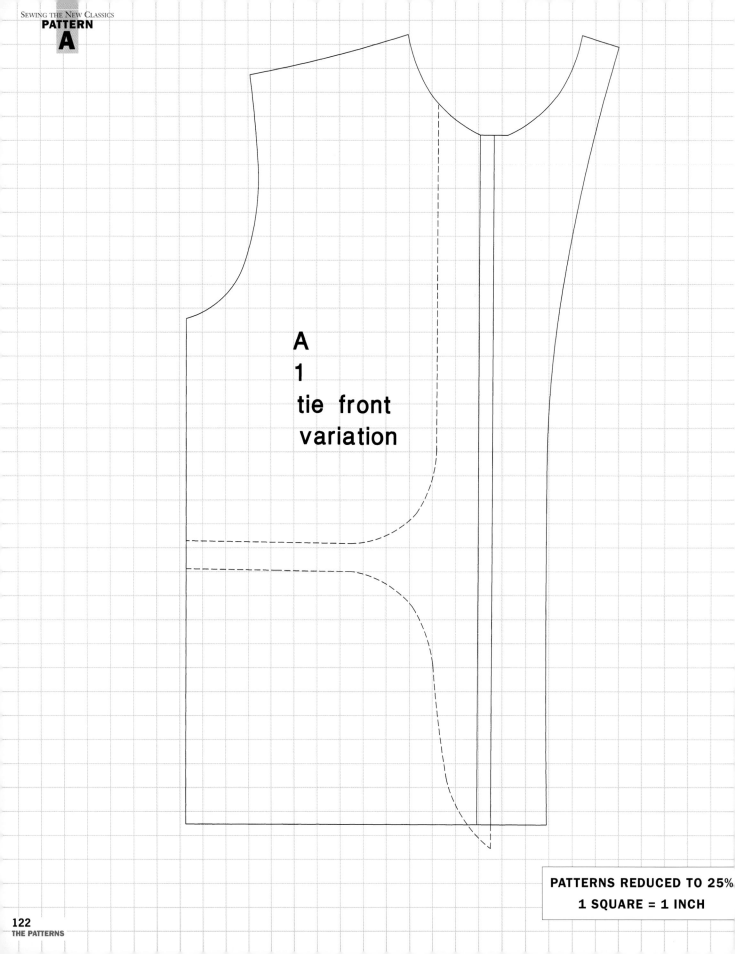

A
1
tie front
variation

PATTERNS REDUCED TO 25%
1 SQUARE = 1 INCH

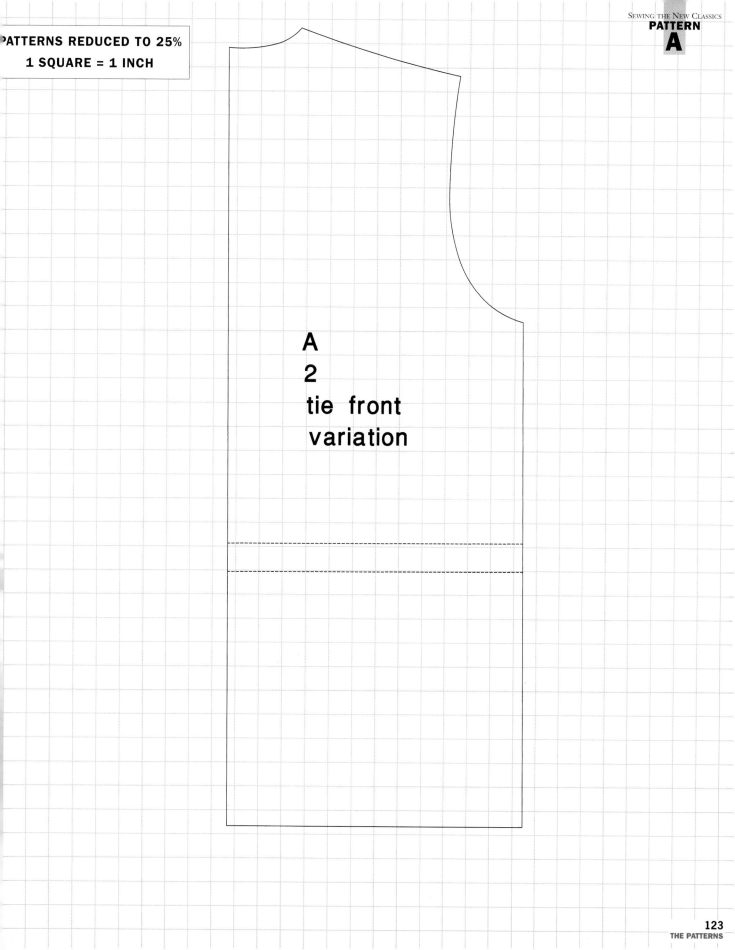

PATTERNS REDUCED TO 25%
1 SQUARE = 1 INCH

A
2
tie front
variation

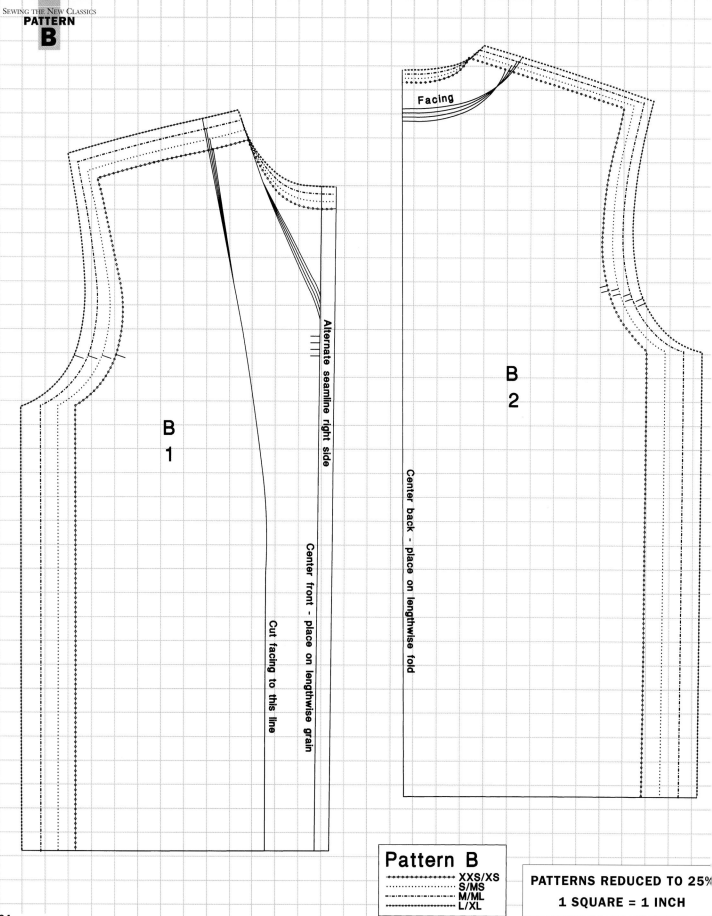

Facing

Alternate seamline right side

B
1

B
2

Center front - place on lengthwise grain

Center back - place on lengthwise fold

Cut facing to this line

Pattern B

- ●━●━●━● XXS/XS
- ·········· S/MS
- ─·─·─·─ M/ML
- ✕━✕━✕ L/XL

PATTERNS REDUCED TO 25%

1 SQUARE = 1 INCH

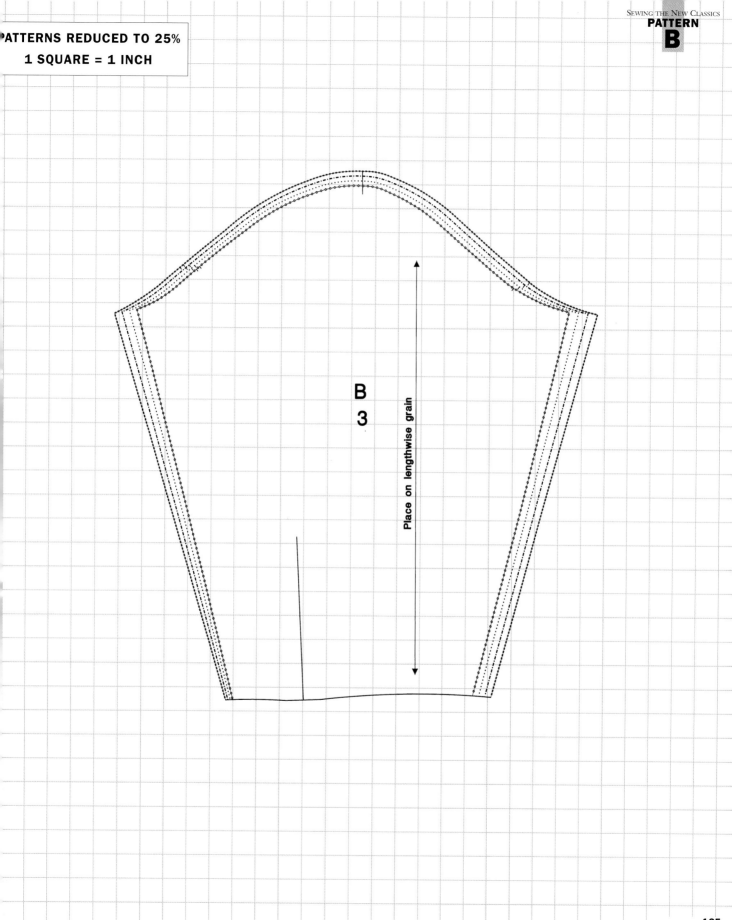

B
3

Place on lengthwise grain

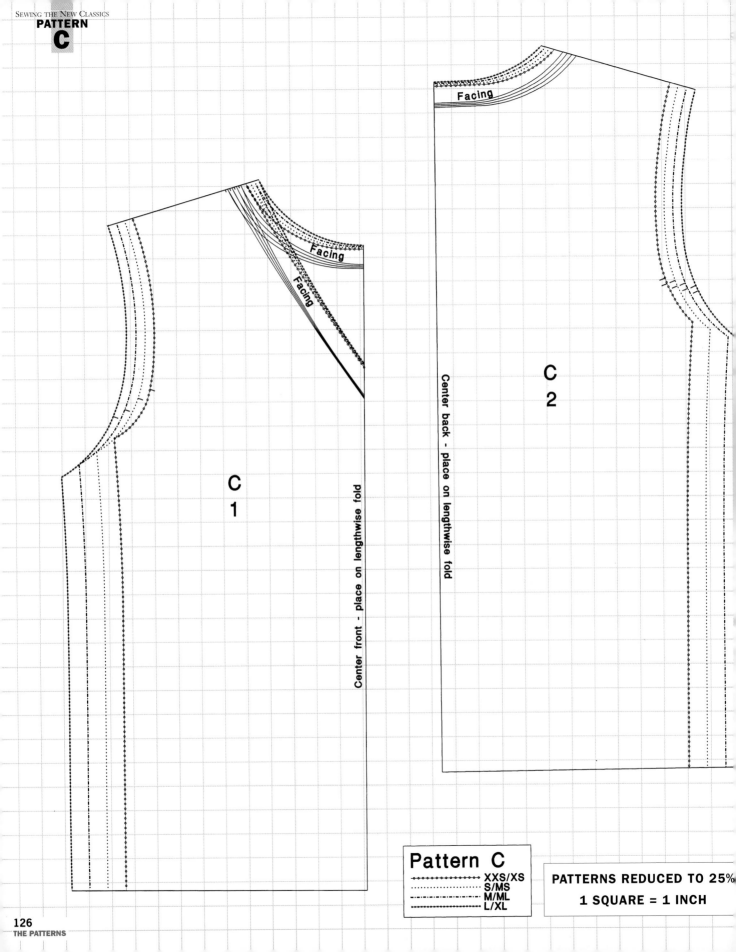

Facing

Facing

Facing

C 1

Center front - place on lengthwise fold

C 2

Center back - place on lengthwise fold

Pattern C

•—•—•—•—•	XXS/XS
············	S/MS
–·–·–·–·–	M/ML
×—×—×—×	L/XL

PATTERNS REDUCED TO 25%

1 SQUARE = 1 INCH

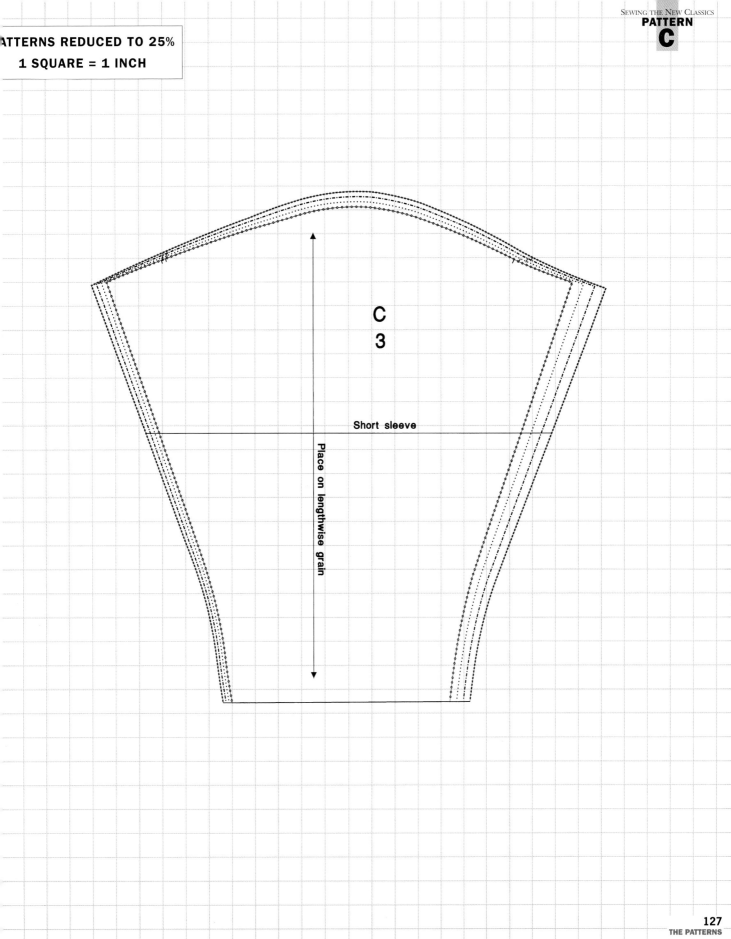

C
3

Short sleeve

Place on lengthwise grain

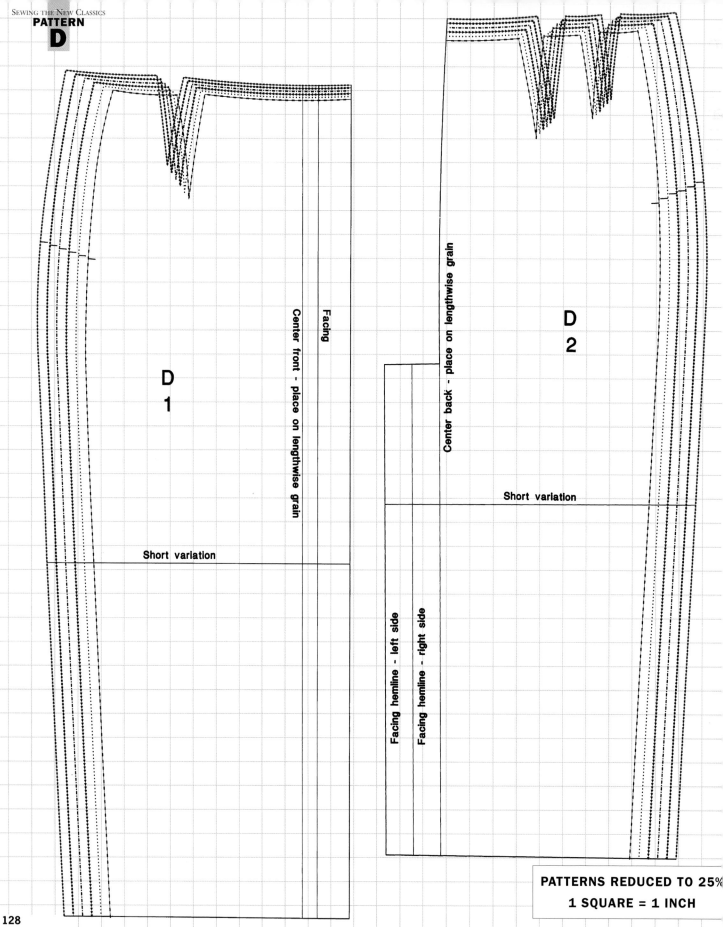

D
1

Facing

Center front - place on lengthwise grain

Short variation

D
2

Center back - place on lengthwise grain

Short variation

Facing hemline - left side

Facing hemline - right side

PATTERNS REDUCED TO 25%

1 SQUARE = 1 INCH

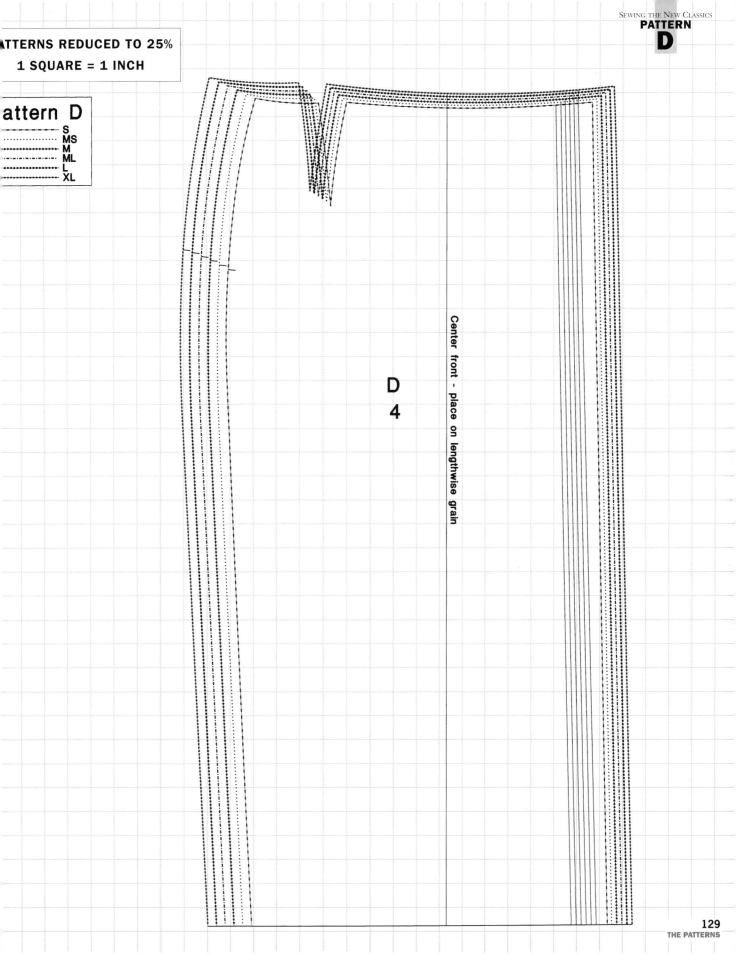

PATTERNS REDUCED TO 25%

1 SQUARE = 1 INCH

Pattern D

········· S
········· MS
·•·•·•·• M
·—·—·— ML
········· L
········· XL

D
4

Center front - place on lengthwise grain

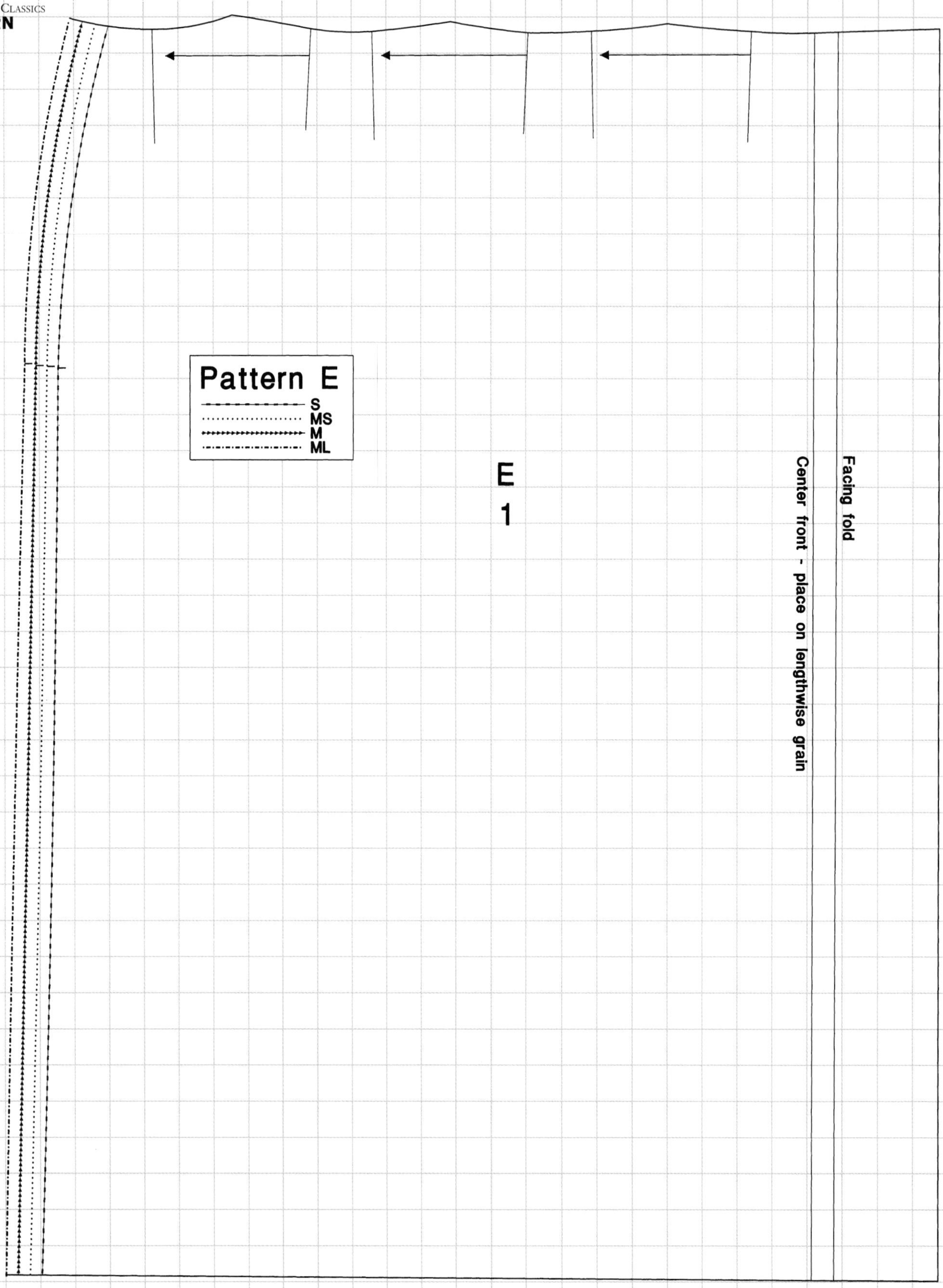

PATTERN
E

Pattern E
- —·— S
- ········· MS
- ▶▶▶▶▶ M
- —··— ML

E
1

Facing fold

Center front - place on lengthwise grain

PATTERNS REDUCED TO 25%
1 SQUARE = 1 INCH

TTERNS REDUCED TO 25%

1 SQUARE = 1 INCH

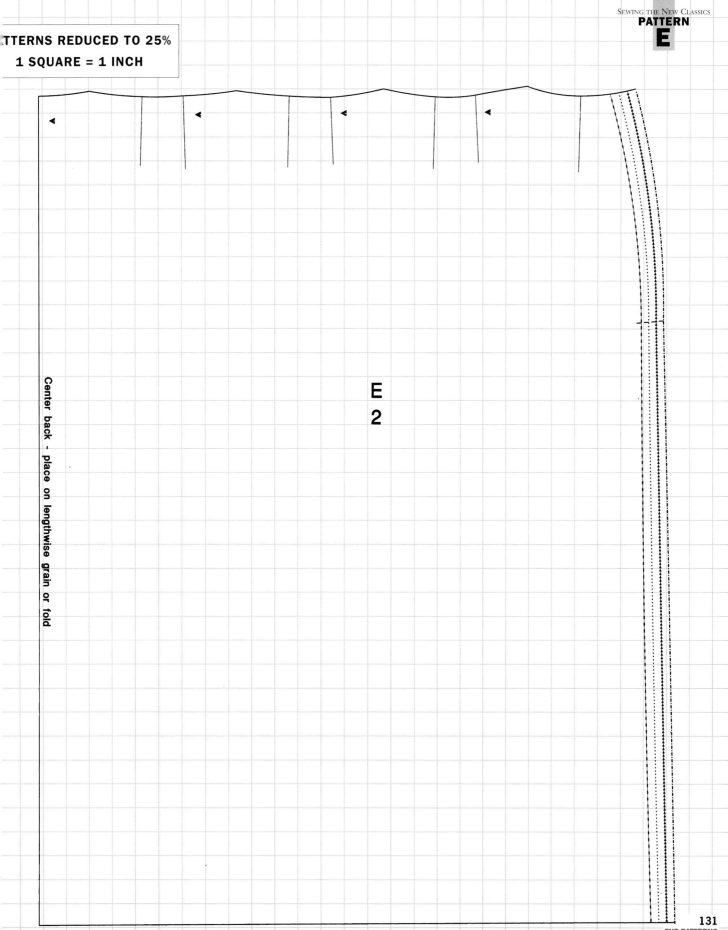

E
2

Center back - place on lengthwise grain or fold

PATTERN

F

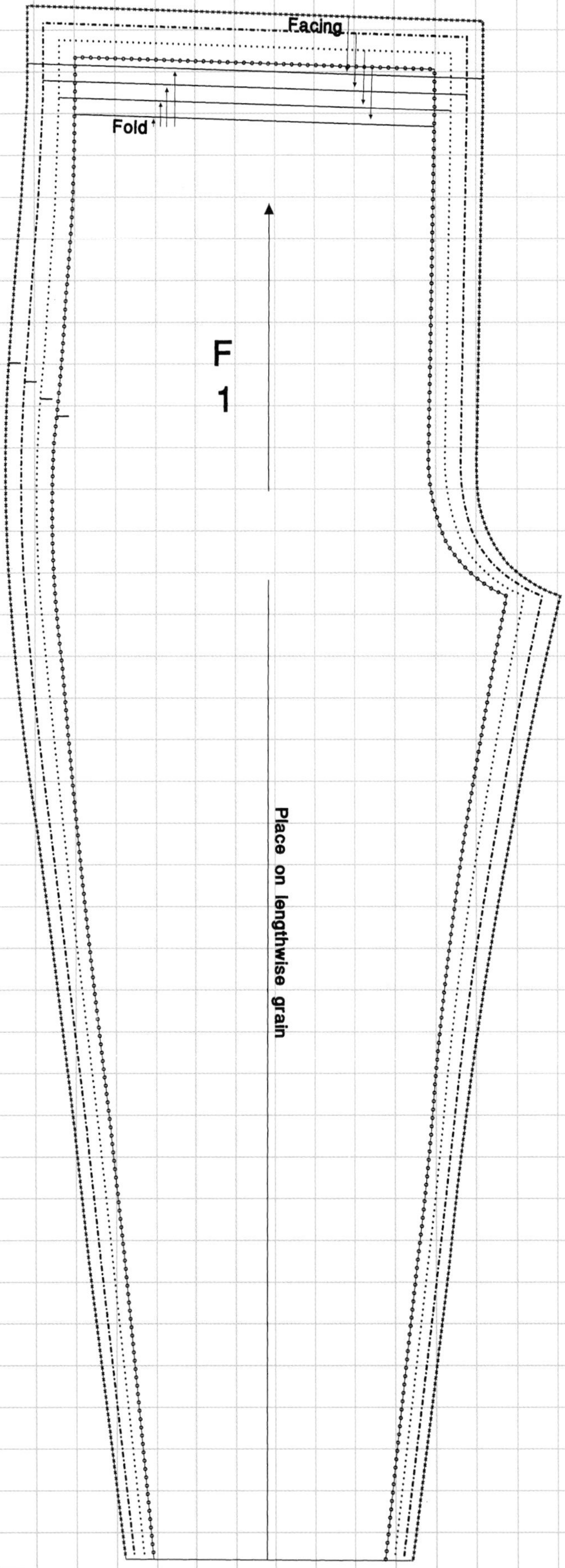
Facing
Fold
F
1
Place on lengthwise grain

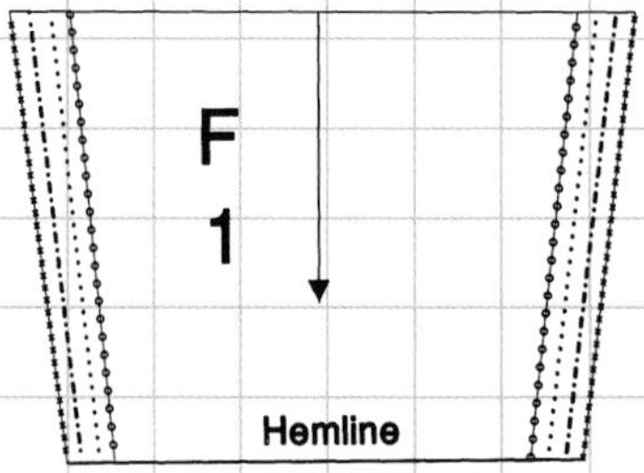
F
1
Hemline

PATTERNS REDUCED TO 25%
1 SQUARE = 1 INCH

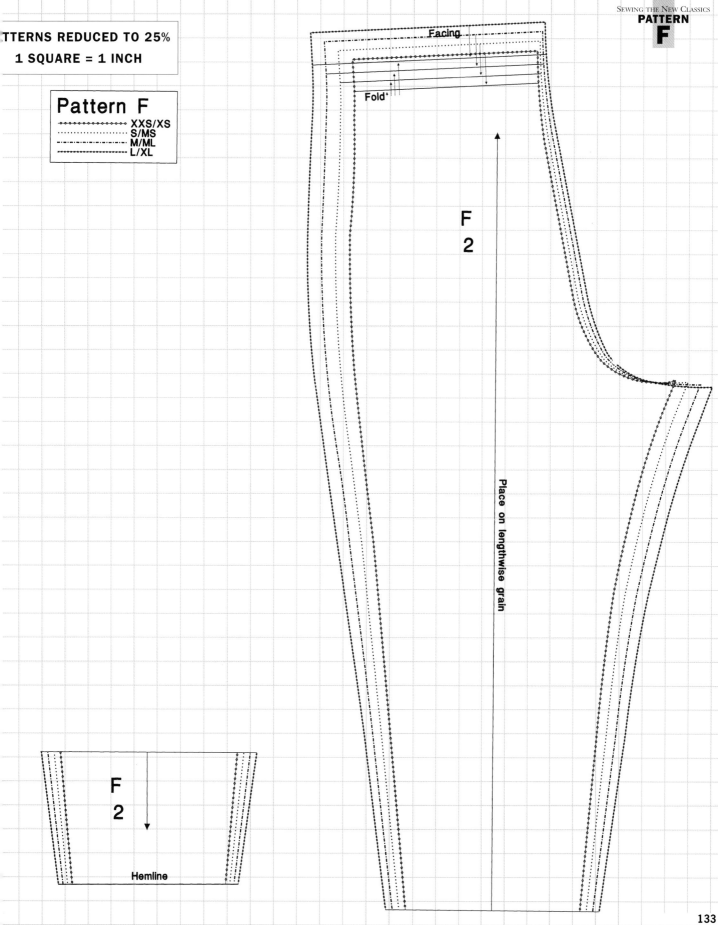

PATTERNS REDUCED TO 25%

1 SQUARE = 1 INCH

Pattern F

- XXS/XS
- S/MS
- M/ML
- L/XL

Facing

Fold

F
2

Place on lengthwise grain

F
2

Hemline

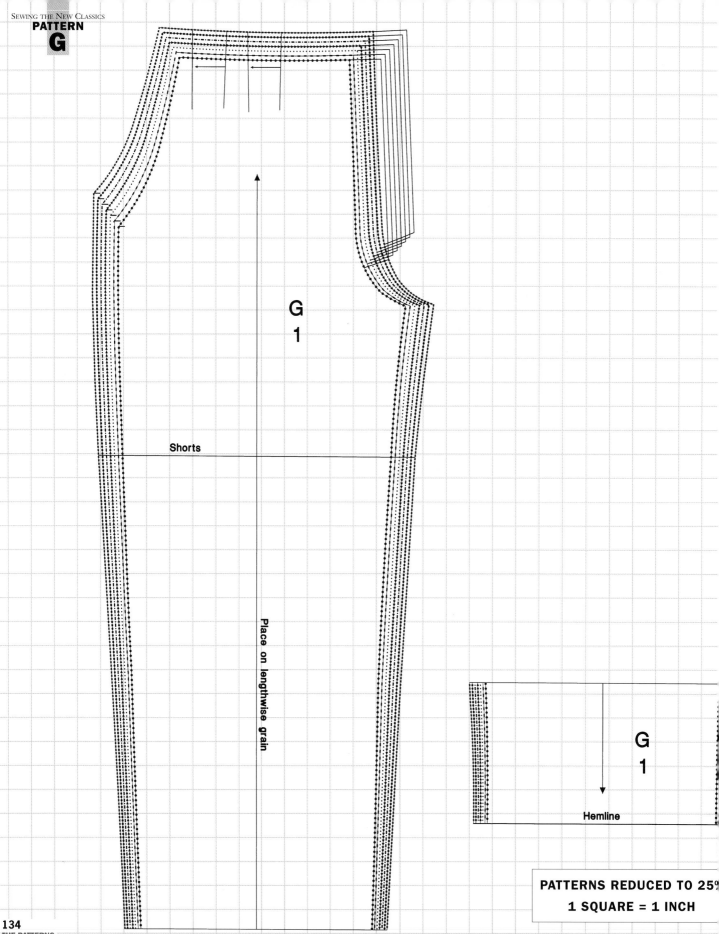

G
1

Shorts

Place on lengthwise grain

G
1

Hemline

**PATTERNS REDUCED TO 25%
1 SQUARE = 1 INCH**

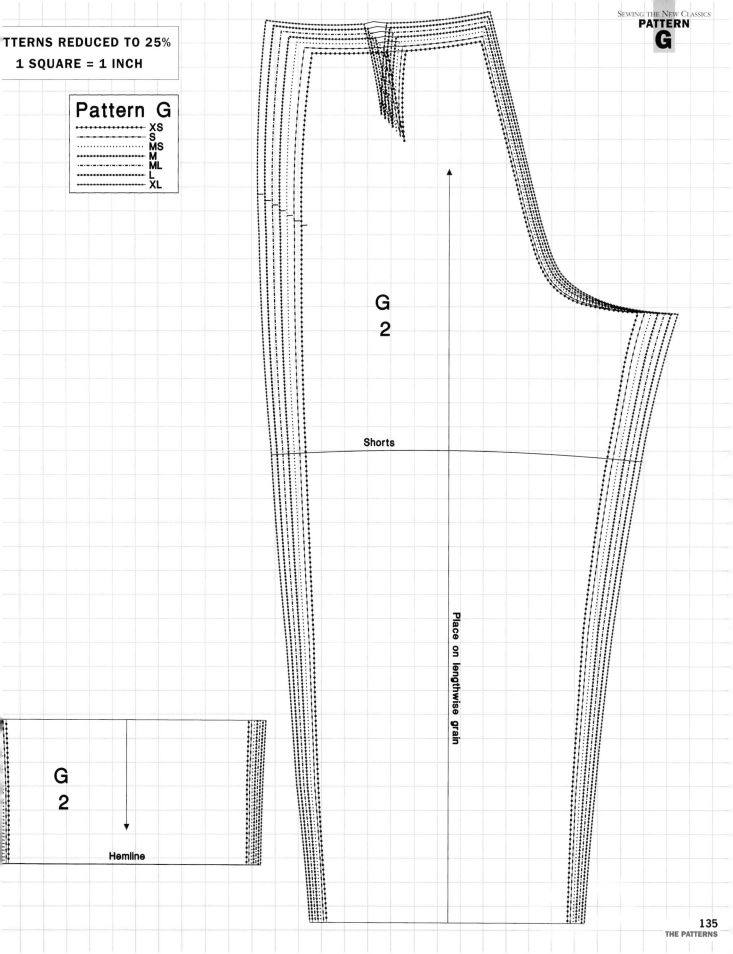

PATTERNS REDUCED TO 25%

1 SQUARE = 1 INCH

Pattern G

••••••••	XS
–•–•–•–	S
••••••••	MS
▸▸▸▸▸▸▸	M
–•–•–•–	ML
••••••••	L
▴▴▴▴▴▴▴	XL

G
2

Shorts

Place on lengthwise grain

G
2

Hemline

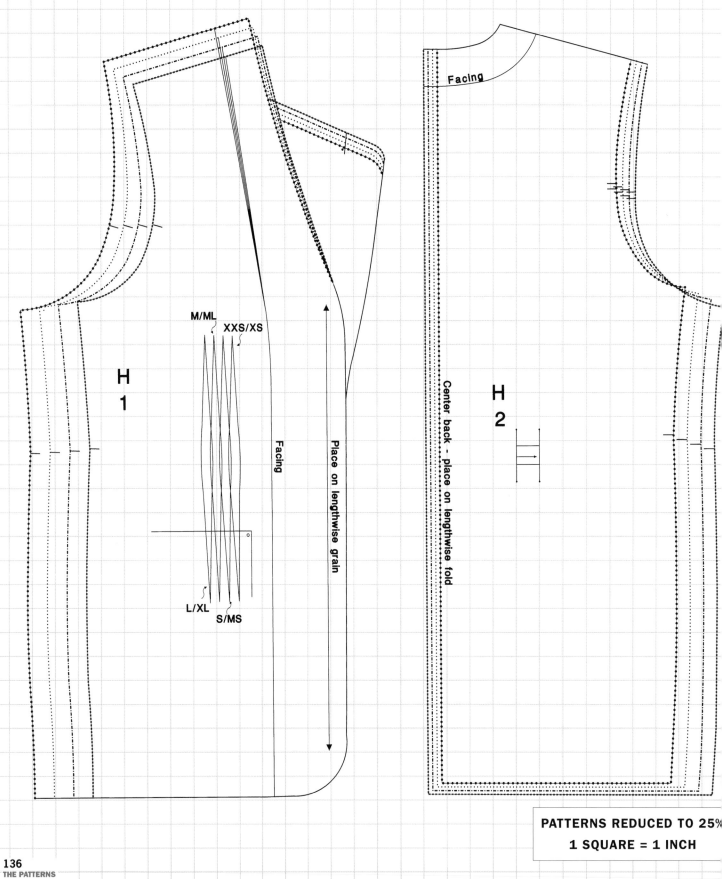

H 1

M/ML

XXS/XS

L/XL

S/MS

Facing

Place on lengthwise grain

H 2

Facing

Center back - place on lengthwise fold

PATTERNS REDUCED TO 25%

1 SQUARE = 1 INCH

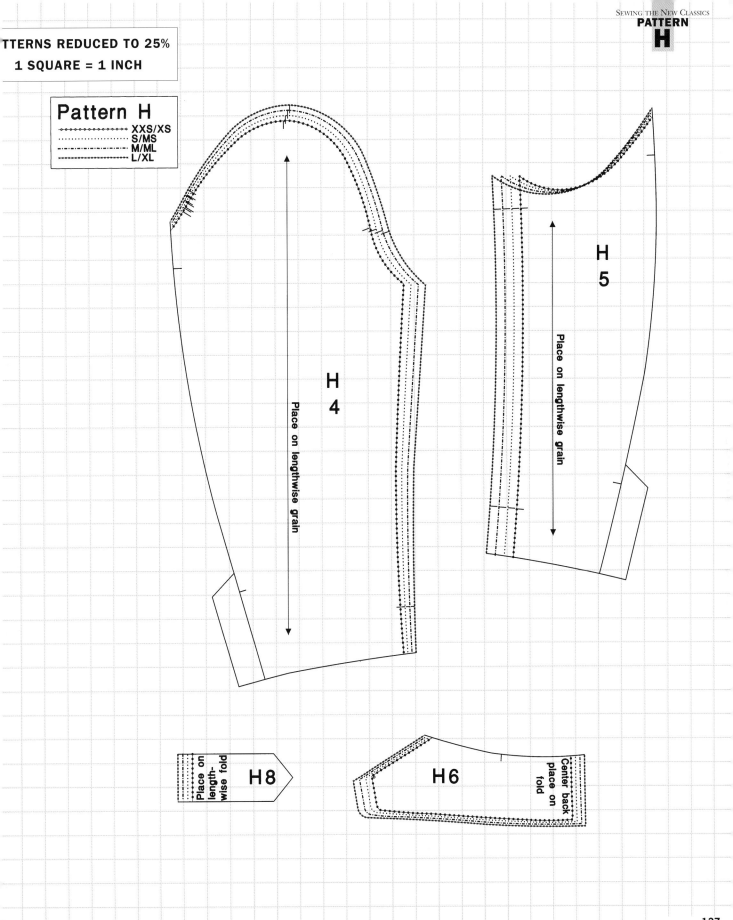

TTERNS REDUCED TO 25%

1 SQUARE = 1 INCH

Pattern H

- •——•——• XXS/XS
- •••••••• S/MS
- •—·—·—· M/ML
- ✕—✕—✕—✕ L/XL

H 4

Place on lengthwise grain

H 5

Place on lengthwise grain

H8

Place on lengthwise fold

H6

Center back place on fold

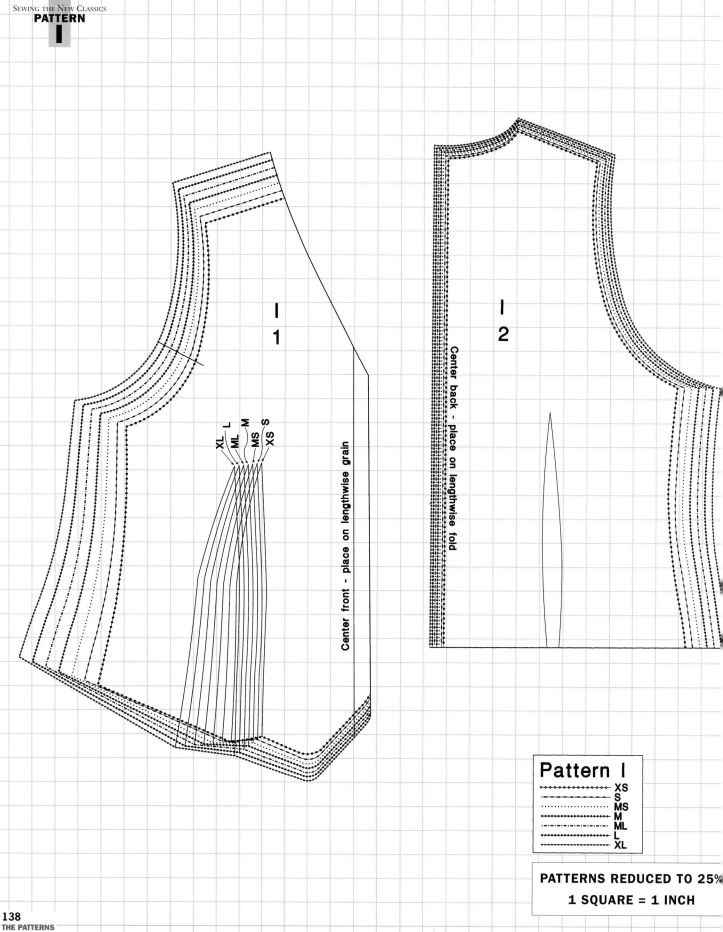

I
1

Center front - place on lengthwise grain

XL
L
ML
M
MS
S
XS

I
2

Center back - place on lengthwise fold

Pattern I

••••••••••••	XS
————————	S
··················	MS
▶▶▶▶▶▶▶▶	M
–·–·–·–·–·	ML
·•·•·•·•·•	L
•••••••••	XL

PATTERNS REDUCED TO 25%

1 SQUARE = 1 INCH

TTERNS REDUCED TO 25%
1 SQUARE = 1 INCH

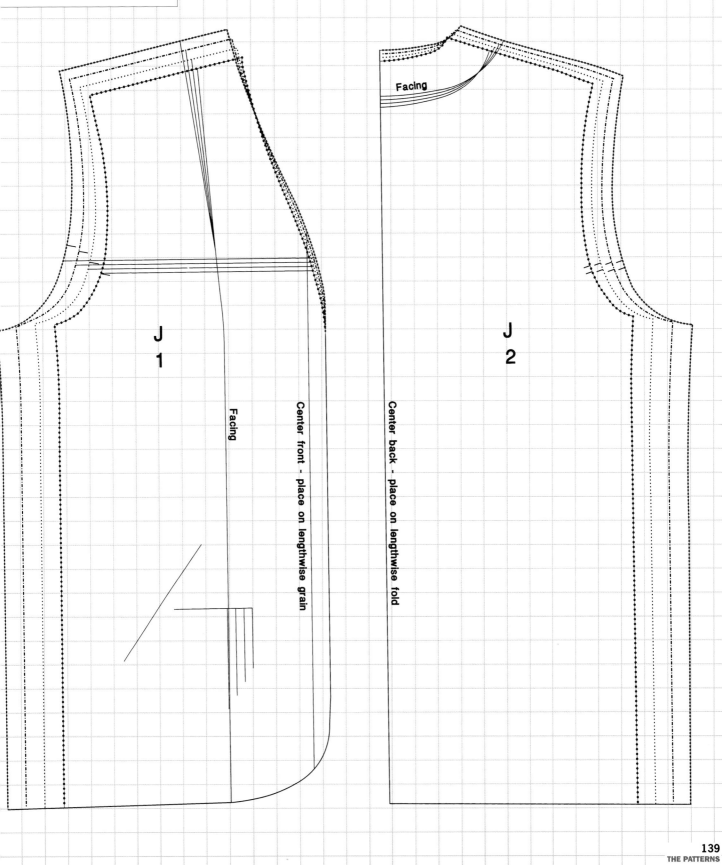

Facing

J
1

Facing

Center front - place on lengthwise grain

Center back - place on lengthwise fold

J
2

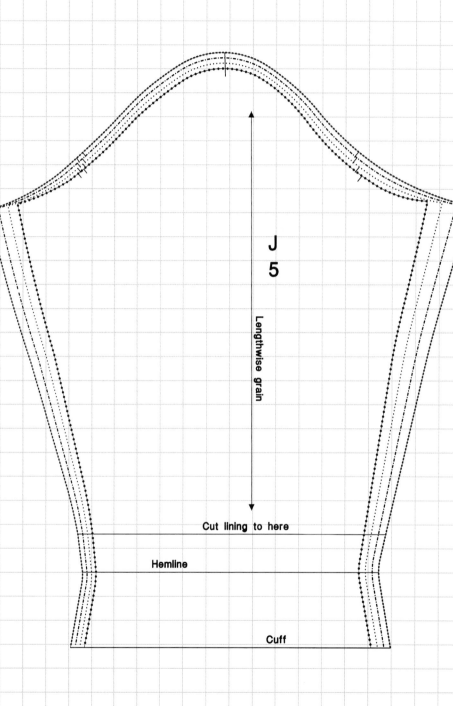

J
5

Lengthwise grain

Cut lining to here

Hemline

Cuff

Pattern J

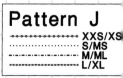

••••••••••••••••	XXS/XS
··················	S/MS
— · — · — · —	M/ML
•••••••••••••••••••	L/XL

PATTERNS REDUCED TO 25%
1 SQUARE = 1 INCH

PATTERNS REDUCED TO 25%

1 SQUARE = 1 INCH

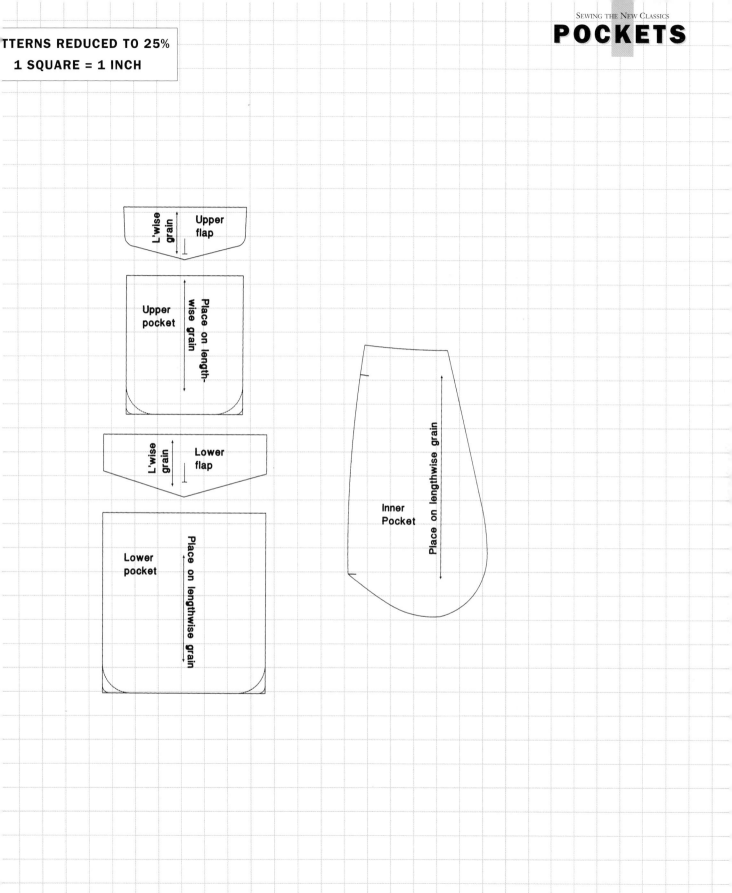

L'wise grain

Upper flap

Upper pocket

Place on length-wise grain

L'wise grain

Lower flap

Lower pocket

Place on lengthwise grain

Inner Pocket

Place on lengthwise grain

acknowledgements

WE ARE GRATEFUL FOR THE HELP OF THESE GOOD PEOPLE:

Evan Bracken, Light Reflections, for the photographs on pages 7, 34, and 93;

Richard Babb, for the photography on page 110;

Elizabeth Lima, who designed and modeled the tunic and skirt shown on pages 7 and 34;

Elma Johnson, for always having time to share her knowledge and her talents, and;

Susan Kieffer, for her tireless pursuit of the most elusive details.

FULL-SIZED PATTERNS AVAILABLE

The producers of Sewing the New Classics *are pleased to offer a Pattern Package that contains all the pattern pieces shown in this section, enlarged to actual size, printed on pattern paper, and ready to use.*

For each Pattern Package send a check or money order for $11.95 – plus postage and handling of $3.50 U.S. ($4.50 Canada), payable to Lark Books.

Or charge to Visa or Mastercard — include card number and expiration date.

SEND TO:

Sewing the New Classics Pattern Package

Lark Books

50 College Street

Asheville, NC 28801

OR CALL TOLL FREE WITHIN THE U.S.
1-800-284-3388 (8:30 - 4:30 E.T.)

Index